SHELTON STATE COI
COLLEGE
JUNIOR COLLEGE DIVISION
LIBRARY

DISCARDED

BX
4406.5
.Z8
S75
1983

Murthy, B. Sriniva-
sa.

      Mother Teresa and
India

W9-BKX-305

DATE DUE		
FEB 1 2 1990		
OCT 0 7 '91	MAR 1 9 2004	
JUL 0 6 1993		
OCT 2 8 1996		
NOV 2 1 1997	SEP 1 4 2017	
SEP 1 4 2000		
APR 2 1 2003	NOV 1 2 2015	

[DISCARDED

MOTHER TERESA

AND

INDIA

B. SRINIVASA MURTHY

LONG BEACH PUBLICATIONS
POST OFFICE BOX 14807
LONG BEACH, CA 90803

Royalties from this book
will go to the
Missionaries of Charity

Copyright © 1983 by B. Srinivasa Murthy.
Library of Congress Catalog Card Number: 82-80522.
International Standard Book Number: 0-941910-00-8.
All Rights Reserved.
Long Beach Publications
Post Office Box 14807
Long Beach, California 90803
Printed in the United States of America

To
all who are striving
to improve the human condition

CONTENTS

Preface
Acknowledgements

PART I: MOTHER TERESA

PART II: INDIA

PREFACE

After seeing a documentary on Mother Teresa in 1973, I was inspired to go to Calcutta to meet Mother Teresa and visit her missionary centers. My friends in India wrote me that Mother Teresa is extremely busy all the time and she travels quite often. If I wanted to meet her in Calcutta, I would have to take a chance that she would be there. In March of 1981, I finally decided to take that chance. Fortunately, I had the privilege of meeting and talking with Mother Teresa during my visit to Calcutta. I asked her about faith, poverty, prayer, abortion and a few personal questions, as well. Mother Teresa very patiently answered all my questions, often with a radiant smile. Meeting Mother Teresa has been a very rewarding spiritual experience and, undoubtedly, my faith has been strengthened. In fact, it has been an unforgettable highlight in my life.

While in Calcutta, two powerful currents of thought kept running through my mind. Firstly, Mother Teresa and her Missionaries of Charity's dedicated life of devotion, simplicity and whole-hearted love and caring for the poorest of the poor has vividly translated the Sermon on the Mount into concrete action. Secondly, the horrible, dehumanizing predicament of the poorest of the poor in the slums of Calcutta deeply stirred my emotions and left me overwhelmed and stunned. Though poverty can be found throughout India, I have never seen such concentrated human misery anywhere else in the country. I began to question why there is so much poverty in India. Can something be done to eradicate poverty or are realistic solutions impossible? As a result of these reflections and my experiences in Calcutta, my mind became set upon translating my thoughts into writing.

After I returned to the United States, I decided to write this book for two reasons: to share Mother Teresa's wonderful spiritual message of serving Jesus through the poorest of the poor with Christian commitment and love, and to analyze the spiritual values of Hinduism and suggest possible solutions to some of India's social problems. Each of us has the moral duty to use our abilities to help our fellowmen and to do what we can to alleviate the problems of hunger and poverty in the world. Indian politicians, the educated and the religious leaders bear the heavy responsibility of tackling the society's social problems.

I am deeply indebted to my friend, Professor Howard Delaney of Loyola Marymount University, Los Angeles, and his wife, Marjorie, who encouraged me to write this book and gave valuable comments on the manuscript. I am also indebted to Mr. Jan H. Lassen, a photographer from Denmark, whom I met at Nirmal Hriday in Calcutta. He generously donated all of the photographs which have been used in this book. A special thank you to Sister Evana Stakor, F.C., of Jesu Ashram, Matigara, India, for her invaluable help. I would also like to thank The Reverend Richard Andersen, pastor of Our Saviour's Lutheran Church in Long Beach, who took keen interest in reading the manuscript and inspired me to stick with the project. This book would not have been completed but for the invaluable help of Mary Jo, who patiently edited, critically evaluated and discussed each chapter.

Additionally, I appreciate the help of: Dorothy Biwer, Director of Special Programs at Marquette University, for having sent the acceptance speech by Mother Teresa at the presentation of the Pere Marquette Discovery Award; James E. Twyman, Director of Public Affairs, Thomas Aquinas College, for having given permission to use Mother Teresa's commencement address; Venkatesha Murthy of Hassan, India, who quickly responded to my request by sending the books I needed from India; Mr. and Mrs. Chandrashekar, with whom I stayed while in Calcutta; Bina Murarka, the editor of India—West, for allowing me to quote from India—West; Reverend Father Robert W. McElroy of the Archdiocese of San Francisco for having sent me a copy of The Monitor, which covered Mother Teresa's speech at St. Mary's Cathedral in detail; and, last but not least, Vivian Davies of Typing Techniques, who did a very fine job of typing the manuscript.

Long Beach, California
January, 1983   B. Srinivasa Murthy

PART I: MOTHER TERESA

CALCUTTA

Visiting Calcutta, even for a few days, is a shocking and unforgettable experience. Arriving at night, a visitor will be dumbfounded by the sight of thousands of homeless people sleeping on the pavement, naked infants lying on jute gunnysacks, and hungry children, carrying babies on their hips, wandering around begging for food. The dim street lights conceal the human quagmire huddled in nooks and corners and tiny kerosine lamps flicker in makeshift tents and tin sheds. People squat on the sidewalks and in the alleys, tending small fires in iron grates or burning chips of wood, dried cow dung, and trash to cook food. The night is filled with a smoky, gloomy haze from the countless street fires combined with auto exhaust and industrial pollution. The whole human drama of existence is played out on the streets. Marriage, sex, child-birth, business, joy and sorrow, disease and death are all experienced in the streets. Privacy is the luxury of those who have a roof over their heads. In the words of the Nobel Laureate poet, Rabind-ranath Tagore, the street dwellers are "eternal tenants in an extortionate world, having nothing of their own."

The utter need and misery of these people is shocking and overwhelming. Although India is not a rich country, I have never seen such concentrated agony of human existence and desolate poverty elsewhere in India.

Walking through the streets of Calcutta is a spine—shaking experience. A tremendous mass of humanity surges through the streets in the sweltering heat and high humidity. Row after row of beggars, lepers, and the blind extend their hands for alms. Stinking garbage is heaped here and there. Police constables in white uniforms and gloves direct the honking cars and busses which barely move through the busy streets. Holy cows and pedestrians obstruct the flow of vehicles and it is an art to drive through the crisscross roads. Trams and busses are jammed with people, who hang in the doorways and stand on the bumpers of the vehicles, sometimes risking their lives to reach their destination.

Women gather around the public water taps, chatting and laughing while waiting their turn to get untreated, brown water from the Hoogly River for cooking and washing. Lean and hungry-looking barefoot men, sweating in the heat and humidity, manually pull rickshaws and run like horses with rhythmic steps to give a ride to fat women shoppers or old office workers. There are roughly 6,000 licensed rickshaw pullers and many thousands who operate without a license. These men do not own their vehicles and are paid a paltry wage of a little over one dollar per day.

There are over 400,000 street dwellers out of Calcutta's nine million population. Some earn their living as street vendors with a rollover capital of a dollar or two in merchandise. Others perform backbreaking labor as coolies, when they are lucky enough to find work. Beggars, lepers, the sick, scrawny destitutes, and the handicapped abound in the slums.

Some of the slums are really tough and dangerous. Each has its own underworld gang leaders, who control the area and claim it as their protected territory. These gangs train vandals, thieves and pickpockets. Even young children are recruited as professional beggars and pickpockets and trained in the survival tactics of life on the street. Trading illicit liquor and prostitution are quite commonplace, as well.

In the Seldah Railway Station area, or in Kidderpore, which are typical slums in Calcutta, it is indeed heartbreaking to witness the height of human misery. I saw an emaciated woman fondly trying to breastfeed a tiny infant, even though her breasts had dried up; lepers, full of open sores and gangrene, extended their hands for alms; and aged men lie like living corpses on the street pavement. Near the markets, the young and the old scavenge for discarded cabbage leaves and rotten fruit and vegetables in the garbage cans, fighting the cows and chasing the crows to get their meager share. Thin, tiny children, half-clad or naked, run around with tears in their eyes searching for something to eat. Some of those who have gone through this immense struggle for bare survival all of their lives simply give up and lie on the pavement. Perhaps they have experientially reached the "existential disgust" and yearn for the last stage of life's voyage. As I saw these tragic sights, the words of Mahatma Gandhi came to my mind: "God Himself dare not appear to a hungry man except in the form of bread."

Dinesh Babu was born in the streets of Calcutta. His father collected newspapers and broken glass bottles from the refuse dumps and sold them to buy food. Dinesh Babu followed in his father's footsteps, collecting and selling glass bottles and newspapers to survive. He said that he was forty-five years old but he looked over sixty. Malnutrition had dried up his last ounce of energy and now he sat under a tree, waiting for his two children, hoping that they would be able to find something to eat in their scavenging. The life of Dinesh Babu in the slum streets is a typical example of the cyclical trap of the chain of bondage passed on from generation to generation, with no possibility of escape. There is only a difference in degree between the poorest of the poor and the emaciated destitutes. The poorest of the poor can fall into the state of destitution at any time, when their energies are drained by illness and malnutrition. Then the only alternative left to them is to count their days to eternity, after having gone through the hellish experience of life.

Of course, not all of Calcutta's population are street dwellers. Wealthy businessmen, aristocrats, and intellectuals live a life of comfort, working in air-conditioned offices and commuting in chauffeur-driven cars. Calcutta is a large industrial center known for its jute, steel plants, shoe factories, chemical industries, and technology. It has a very rich cultural heritage of poets, novelists, artists, religious reformers, Hindu philosophers, and social and political leaders. The city has produced internationally famous personalities, such as Nobel Laureate Rabindranath Tagore, Ravi Shanker, Satyajit Ray, and prominent religious figures, such as Ramakrishna Paramahansa, Swami Vivekananda, Paramahansa Yogananda, and the Nobel Laureate Mother Teresa, to name a few. The people of Calcutta are proud of their intellectual and spiritual heritage and Calcutta is a dynamic, exciting and stimulating city if one looks at the variety of intellectual and cultural activities available.

On Chowrunghee Street, an exclusive shopping area, beautiful women stroll in and out of the shops, adorned in expensive sarees and gold jewelry. On Park Street, the luxurious hotels and nightclubs serve lavish dinners and entertainment in the Continental style. The cost of just one night's meal and entertainment could keep a slum family fed for months! The rich are either insensitive to the plight of the poor or they have simply become immune to the misery of the masses over the years. Higgle-haggling for bargain prices with the railway station porters and street vendors is a familiar scene. The rich won't even pay wages generously for labor and services rendered. I was told by one Bengali: "When the well-to-do employ servants, they demand hard work from them but, in turn, the pay the servants receive is meager. The services of the poor are undervalued and there is no respect for them as persons. Those who are in good positions financially think that it is the duty of the poor to serve them and their hard labor is taken for granted." In fact, such an attitude is common throughout India. Although it is the mark of economic prudence to look for "bargains," the exploitation of our fellow suffering human beings is unethical and unjustified.

Calcutta's growth has not been planned; hence, the unchecked expansion reflects the influx of people over the years. Prominent highrise buildings and modern architecture rise out of the slums; spacious bungalows of aristocrats have been built alongside large colonial style mansions; old buildings, which are remnants of the British colonial empire, crumple in the last stages of decay; and, alas, slums are everywhere. In other Indian cities, the slums are generally located in the outskirts of the main business centers. But, in Calcutta, the destitute live even on the sidewalks in front of the mansions of the wealthy.

What is the origin of the unmanageable problems found in Calcutta? How did so many impoverished people end up in the slums and why can't the government deal with their needs? Unfortunately, there are no simple answers to these questions. However, a few facts will shed some light on the complexity of the situation.

After India became independent from British rule in 1947, the province of Bengal was divided into East and West Bengal. East Bengal became part of Pakistan and, in 1973, attained the status of an independent nation, Bangladesh, wherein the majority of citizens are of the Moslem faith. At the time of the partition in 1947, as well as when Bangladesh was established as a country, millions of Hindu refugees poured into Calcutta, adding an even greater population burden to the already overcrowded city. Hundreds of people still come to Calcutta every day to start a new life. Landless agricultural workers and the unskilled and unemployed migrate to the city in search of jobs. The continuous wave of new migrants create more unemployment and the newcomers usually end up in the slums. In addition, Calcutta is often ravaged by heavy monsoons and floods, creating immense damage to property and leaving thousands homeless. During the drought years in West Bengal, people also pour into Calcutta from surrounding areas with the hope that it may be easier to get food and survive.

The central government in New Delhi and the state government of West Bengal have struggled to combat the problems and to improve the city but their efforts have been miniscule compared with the magnitude of the human need. Not only has poverty infested the city but turbulent social and political unrest shakes Calcutta time and time again. The slums are the stronghold of ultra-radical Marxists and a violent anarchist group, known as the Naxalites. Strikes, violent agitations and sit-ins, organized and instigated by these groups, are commonplace in the city. The political uproar from the masses is unpredictable and often leads to spontaneous violence and killing. In Calcutta, it is difficult to surmise what may happen from one day to the next.

In this rich, turbulent, and depressing city, Mother Teresa dreamed of serving the poorest of the poor. With unshakable faith and tremendous courage, she and her Missionaries of Charity have been striving incessantly to uplift the destitute from the dehumanizing conditions which surround them, affirming that "they . . . and you and me . . have been created to love and be loved; that they are our brothers and sisters; that they are somebody . . . they are Jesus."[1]

MOTHER TERESA

In a world torn with greed, selfishness and oppression, it is an immmense joy and inspiration to find a spiritual giant like Mother Teresa of Calcutta. The hungry, the sick, the outcast, the abandoned children, the lonely and unwanted in the teeming ghettos of Calcutta, all find the inspiration of God's love and compassionate care through Mother Teresa and her Missionaries of Charity.

Wherever Mother Teresa goes in Calcutta, people throng to see her. Some try to touch her feet, thus showing traditional Hindu veneration and respect and bestowing upon her all their love and gratitude. To see her gracious, loving smile, even for a moment, leaves an indelible impression of peace and serenity. Her dynamism, unfathomable reservoir of energy, and patience in listening and responding to problems is remarkable. She has been called "a living saint" and "the saint of the gutters" by those who know of her work, irrespective of their political, cultural or religious backgrounds. Her life has clearly demonstrated that, with faith, good will and love, we can do wonders in uplifting the human condition from wretchedness to human dignity and from apathy, deliberate callousness and cynicism to the heights of sublime spirituality.

What makes Mother Teresa's personality so magnetic and powerful, in spite of her utter simplicity and humility? Why do people around the globe come to visit and participate in her work? Why do they have the highest genuine love and respect for this nun? The answer is powerfully simple. She is emulating the life of Jesus Christ.

Professor John Sannes, the chairman of the Nobel Committee, aptly described Mother Teresa's philosophy of life during the Nobel Prize ceremony in 1979. "A hallmark of her work has been respect for the individual human being, for his or her dignity and innate value. The loneliest, the most wretched and the dying have at her hands received compassion without condescension, based on reverence for man . . . In the eyes of the Norwegian Nobel Committee constructive efforts to do away with hunger and poverty, and to ensure for men and women a safer and better world community in which to develop, should be inspired by the spirit of Mother Teresa, by respect for the worth and dignity of the individual human being."[1] He further stressed that Mother Teresa's message reaches something innate in every human mind, planting the seed for good. "If this were not the case the world would be deprived of hope and work for peace would have little meaning."[2] Echoing the same notion, the former president of the World Bank, Robert MacNamara, said: "Mother Teresa deserves the Nobel Prize because she promotes peace in the most fundamental manner, by her confirmation of the inviolability of human dignity."[3]

Mother Teresa accepted the Nobel Peace Prize "in the name of the hungry, of the naked, of the homeless, of the blind, of the lepers, of all those who feel unwanted, unloved, uncared for throughout society . . . Though I'm personally unworthy, I'm grateful and I'm very happy to receive it (for the world's poor). Our poor people are great people, a very lovable people. They don't need our pity and sympathy. They need our understanding love and they need our respect."[4] We need to demonstrate to the poor, she continued, that "they are somebody to us, that they too have been created with the same loving hand of God, to love and be loved."[5]

Mother Teresa's spiritual journey of faith and service is incredible. How did this simple nun become the leader and inspiration of a worldwide organization of religious dedicated to serving the poorest of the poor? The following narration of the beginnings of the Order of the Missionaries of Charity is based upon my conversations with Sister Evana, a Yugoslavian missionary who has been working with lepers in the Darjeeling District of West Bengal for almost half a century,[6] as well as conversations with nuns in Calcutta and Bombay, and with my friends in Calcutta.

Agnes Gonxha Bojaxhiu was born on August 27, 1910 in Skopje, Albania, which is now a part of Yugoslavia. As a young girl, Agnes read about the Bengali missions through the newsletters of the Yugoslavian Jesuit priests. Until the 1930's, India was a very prime area for sowing the seeds of Christianity, especially among the lower castes, the tribes, and the untouchables. The rigid caste system of Hindu society provided a splendid opportunity for their conversion, thereby giving them a life of dignity and self-respect as Christians. Large numbers of missionaries, primarily from France, Belgium, Britain, Italy, Yugoslavia, Denmark, and the U.S.A., began missionary vocations in India. They dedicated their lives to spreading the gospel through educational institutions, hospitals, orphanages, and missions in remote areas.

Agnes Bojaxhiu became enthusiastic about the Indian missions and she decided to dedicate her life to serving Christ and spreading the gospel.

She joined the Order of Our Lady of Loretto in
Ireland and then came to India. After her novi-
tiate training in Darjeeling, she took her vows as
a nun. Mother Teresa began her first spiritual
vocation as a teacher at a high school run by the
Loretto sisters at Entally in Calcutta. Mother
Teresa taught there for about twenty years and was
also the school principal.

Educating children of the well-to-do and middle
class, however, did not satisfy Mother Teresa. The
destitute and the hungry, whom she had seen over
the years in Calcutta, must have had a tremendous
impact upon her. In contrast, the life at the
convent was secure, comfortable and well-provided.
While traveling to a retreat in Darjeeling by train
in 1946, Mother Teresa received "a call within a
call. The message was clear, I was to leave the
convent and help the poor, while living among
them."[7]

Normally, we conclude that anyone who has dedicated themselves to a spiritual life has already
received God's direction, once and for all, and
that their life is set in order. But in actuality
it may not be so. God's direction and revelation
is a continuing process. God purifies the heart
and mind as long as we seek Him earnestly and allow
Him to guide our lives by listening to His inspiration. Only those who are spiritually alert will
hear His message.

What could this nun do, alone in the streets of
the ghastly slums of Calcutta? How would she leave
the convent and the life to which she had become
accustomed? In God's providence, everything is
possible with faith because "faith is the assurance
of things hoped for, the conviction of things not
seen." (Hebrews 11:1, RSV) Mother Teresa received
permission from the bishop of Calcutta to live

outside the convent and to serve the poor in the streets. Alone, armoured with indelible faith, she walked through the slums determined to help the poorest of the poor. Christ was her only guide and companion.

Mother Teresa began working in Moti Jheel, a slum area not far from the Loretto school where she had taught. She wore a white cotton saree, bordered in blue, with a crucifix visibly fastened on her left shoulder. This simple dress was later to become the habit of the Missionaries of Charity. Initially, Mother's work centered around teaching the street children, caring for the destitute and visiting the sick in hospitals. She lived with the generous Bengali Catholic family of Mr. Michael Gomes.

A former student of Mother Teresa's at the Loretto high school, Subhasini Das, joined her and renounced everything to dedicate her life to serving Christ in the poor. She was Mother's first postulant. Subhasini Das took the name of Agnes, which was Mother Teresa's baptismal name. During the years in which Mother Teresa and Sister Agnes lived with the Gomes family, quite a few sisters joined them and innumerable lay people and religious in Calcutta contributed to their work with the destitute. Sister Evana told me of a beautiful incident which took place in Calcutta during the early years of Mother Teresa's service. One day Mother Teresa was surprised to see a young man cleaning the wounds of a leper. She asked him what his name was and he replied, "Christo Das," which means "servant of Christ." Christo Das has been one of the pioneers in the selfless service of the Missionaries of Charity.

Mother Teresa visualized starting her own order of nuns to be known as the Missionaries of Charity.

Her dream became a reality in 1950 when the pope gave permission for her to organize the new religious order. A chart on the wall of Mother Teresa's small office sums up the aims and ideals of the Missionaries of Charity. "Our particular mission is to labor at the salvation and sanctification of the poorest of the poor . . . nursing the sick and the dying destitute . . . gathering and teaching little street children . . . giving shelter to the abandoned . . . caring for the unwanted, the unloved and the lonely . . . In so doing we prove our love for Jesus."[8] In one of her speeches, Mother Teresa has further elaborated: "That's why our sisters and brothers take the vow to love Christ with undivided love and chastity, through the freedom of poverty, in total surrender, in obedience. That fourth vow of giving wholehearted free service to the poorest of the poor is that fruit of chastity, that fruit of that undivided love for Christ. Because it is in them, in the lonely, the unwanted, that He is."[9]

Mother Teresa's dedicated service became well-known in the community, especially among Catholic priests and laity, as a result of which the Order of the Missionaries of Charity steadily increased in numbers. The Archbishop of Calcutta, Albert D'Souza, assisted Mother Teresa in moving to a larger residence. I knew Archbishop D'Souza from the time he became the Bishop of Mysore in South India and he always expressed great concern and generosity in helping those in need. The Missionaries of Charity's new residence, located at 54-A Lower Circular Road, became popularly known as the "mother house" and is still the headquarters of the order.

Mother Teresa was deeply moved by the appalling and dehumanizing conditions in which people died on the streets without food, water or care. The

emaciated and terminally ill lay helplessly in
their own waste, often covered with maggots and
rotting flesh. With God's guidance, overcoming
insurmountable obstacles, Mother Teresa was able to
establish Nirmal Hriday (Home for the Dying) in
1954 in Kalighat, after the municipality of Calcutta donated the vacant guest house adjacent to
the famous Hindu Temple of Kali. Another crying
need to which Mother Teresa responded was the
plight of abandoned infants who were left on the
streets to die. She established Shishu Bhavan
(Chindren's Home) to care for abandoned and
orphaned babies. These two centers became proto-
types of the Missionaries of Charity's concrete
spiritual service and similar centers were established in many other cities throughout India.

Caring for lepers has also been a primary and
significant ministry of Mother Teresa's from the
early days of her work in the slums. There are
thousands of lepers in Calcutta and more than three
million lepers in India. These unfortunate people
are shunned by society because of the widespread
belief and fear that leprosy is contagious. A
cruel fate awaits anyone unlucky enough to be
stricken with the dreaded disease, for even the
closest and dearest family members will avoid them.
More often than not, the lepers voluntarily leave
their homes and end up in the slums, far away from
family and friends.

While I was a student in India, I knew an
educated, talented and economically prosperous
individual who was in his mid-fifties when he
contracted leprosy. The whole family was over-
whelmed with grief and panic that they would not be
able to arrange the marriages of his five daughters. No one would marry the girls out of fear
they they may be carriers of the disease. The
father realized the probable future impediments to

his daughters' marriages, so, to keep his illness a secret, he committed suicide, hoping that his death would ease his childrens' predicament. After a few years, the family was able to arrange for the marriage of all five daughters since only the immediate family and a few intimate friends knew the tragic facts.

Seeing the sad plight of lepers and recognizing their need for medical and spiritual assistance, Mother Teresa established a leper colony known as Shanti Nagar (City of Peace) near Calcutta. In Shanti Nagar, the lepers are provided with housing and medical care. Mother Teresa has successfully implemented programs to teach the lepers job skills like carpentry, housing construction, weaving and other handicrafts, thereby giving the lepers a chance to feel that they too are persons who can live with dignity and contribute to the community. Mother Teresa never tires of urging the lepers to be self-sufficient in whatever ways they can and their efforts will be rewarded with new hope, peace and joy. Today, the Missionaries of Charity have many centers in Calcutta to serve leprosy patients, including mobile clinics to treat less serious cases.

The Indian government is also struggling to overcome the problems of leprosy through medical care, health education, and improved public sanitation. There are approximately 3,200,000 cases of leprosy in India, of which 800,000 cases are infectious. A major thrust of the National Leprosy Advisory Committee is to educate the public regarding the facts that leprosy can be cured in the early stages and that eighty percent of the leprosy cases are not contageous. The 1980-81 national budget provided thirty-five million rupees to the Central Health Sector to combat the disease. India has 382 leprosy control units, 430 urban leprosy

centres, 231 leprosy homes and hospitals, 190
temporary hospital wards, and 6,590 SETS (Survey,
Education and Treatment Centers). Additionally,
eight international and forty national voluntary
agencies are providing personnel and financial
assistance for the lepers.[10] The Indian government
has assisted the Missionaries of Charity in carrying on their work, as Mother Teresa has acknow-
ledged: " . . . the government has given us land in
every state where we work to rehabilitate the
lepers. This problem of leprosy is very big in
India."[11]

In the year 1963, Mother Teresa established the
Order of the Brothers of the Missionaries of
Charity for lay Catholic men who aspire to share
the practical vision of serving Christ in the poor,
following the same religious principles as the
Sisters of the Missionaries of Charity. A long-
time associate of Mother Teresa, Brother Andrew,
became the superior general of the Brothers of the
Missionaries of Charity. In Calcutta, the brothers
are in charge of many homes for dying destitutes
and they operate a large leper colony in Titagarh,
where approximately 5,000 leper families are re-
habilitated. Additionally, the brothers teach slum
families the art of weaving and other practical
handicrafts. The Brothers of the Missionaries of
Charity maintain a home for the physically handicapped and mentally retarded children and operate a
huge indoor psychiatric hospital in Antara, Calcutta. They teach the abandoned street children to
read and write, as well, by conducting classes on
the slum sidewalks.

Mother Teresa's centers in Calcutta were founded upon tremendous hardship, dedicated effort and
vigilant prayer. People of many religious backgrounds and all walks of life, Indians and foreign-
ers, the poor and the rich, as well as inter-

national charitable organizations, all generously
contributed their services, cash donations, buildings and food supplies toward Mother Teresa's work.
The Missionaries of Charity's accomplishments are
an outstanding testimony which demonstrate that, if
we singlemindedly pursue good deeds and unselfish
service, the hand of God will be there to bless our
efforts. Miracles do happen when we demonstrate to
God our faith, dedication, good will and love. As
Mother Teresa so aptly puts it, "Love one another
as you love Jesus. Whatever we do to each other we
do to Him . . . Not by doing the big things, but by
doing the little things with great love."[12]

Even though Mother Teresa is modest and humble,
saying that all is God's work and that she is an
"ordinary woman," her missionary enterprise and
achievements are astounding! Just as financial
entrepreneurs know how to invest, where to invest,
and how to mobilize their resources to achieve
grand financial success; likewise, Mother Teresa
has utilized practical entrepreneurial genius in
setting up service centers around the world with
astonishing success. She can size up a slum,
intuitively judge the needs of the people, and
mobilize self-help programs in the area. Mother
Teresa must have splendid managerial capacity and
prudential wisdom, for such achievements are impossible for theoretical idealists. Just as
financial wizards have faith, vision, knowledge and
singleminded perseverance to achieve their goals in
the material world; likewise, Mother Teresa has
indomitable faith in Jesus, the vision to meet the
needs of the destitute, knowledge of how to utilize
the given resources, and strict spiritual discipline. Just as big corporations have their
chains of business establishments, so has Mother
Teresa established her spiritual chain of service
centers worldwide. In the former, "profit" is the
watchword; but in the latter, is the "giving," in

the sense of giving unselfish service, love and dignity to our suffering fellow men.

Today, the Missionaries of Charity have more than one hundred centers in India. Apart of Calcutta, the major centers are in Bombay (one in Byculla and another in Bandra), New Delhi, Agra, Darjeeling, Coimbatore, Madras, Patna, Hyderabad, Jemshedpur, and Bangalore. Wherever the Missionaries of Charity have been invited to open a center and provided with the basic material support, Mother Teresa has willingly accepted the invitation to serve the poor in the name of Jesus, after being convinced of the genuine need in the area.

For the first time in the history of all Indian churches, a religious order is sending missionaries to other parts of the world. The Missionaries of Charity are serving the poor in fifty-two countries with 213 houses. There are approximately 2,000 sisters and 250 brothers of the Missionaries of Charity, as well as an international association of lay coworkers numbering over forty thousand. Their service centers can be found in Britain, West Germany, Italy, Spain, France, the United States, Mexico, Tanzania, Kenya, Jordan, Lebanon, Egypt and Australia. Last year, Vatican Radio broadcast that Mother Teresa thinks that there is every possibility of sending some nuns to work in mainland China. She commented that "we are trying to send some sisters, but we must still pray . . . Nothing is impossible." What spiritual stamina! In spite of her enormous successes, Mother Teresa never claims an iota of personal credit. "Let there be no pride or vanity in our work. Our work is God's work. Let the work remain His. Pray for us that we don't spoil His work."[13]

Westerners might wonder why Mother Teresa has opened centers in their metropolitan cities. Some people are of the opinion that, in the United States and Europe, there are ample opportunities for poor people to uplift themselves economically, if only they would work hard and be frugal. They contend that those who are impoverished are basically lazy and have become accustomed to being parasites of the generous social welfare system. I have often heard the comment that there are no dying destitutes lying on the streets of the western cities, as found in Calcutta, and Mother Teresa and her Missionaries of Charity could do more in Calcutta itself. I posed some of these questions in a letter and one of the sisters of the Missionaries of Charity wrote from Calcutta in reply: "We work not just for the materially poor, but also for the spiritually poor. In fact, most of our work in the western countries is with the spiritually poor . . . the lonely, the alcoholic, the drug addict, shut-ins, etc." In her speech at Marquette University in Milwaukee, Wisconsin, Mother Teresa expressed the same sentiments:

> Right here in the United States, I'm sure you know better than I do, there are many poor people that need love and compassion; that need your hands to serve them; that need your hearts to love them. There are many shut-ins that have forgotten what is love and what is human touch, and it is they that are hungry for love. People are not hungry just for bread, they are hungry for love. People are not naked only for a piece of cloth; they are naked for that human dignity. People are not only homeless for a room made of bricks; but they are homeless—— being rejected, unwanted, unloved. Jesus says: "Love as I have loved you; I have wanted you."[14]

In June 1982, while addressing more than four thousand people at St. Mary's Cathedral during San Francisco's celebration of the 800th birthday of its patron saint, Francis of Assisi, Mother Teresa stated that the hunger for human love is more urgent than the hunger for food and she pointed out the terrible pain and loneliness of being unwanted. "The hunger is not just for bread and rice, but to be loved, to be someone." Again, in Santa Paula, California, while addressing the students of Thomas Aquinas College, she commented that in the United States there is no starvation as in India, where people sometimes die of hunger, but in the U.S., on the contrary, "there is a terrible hunger of love, a terrible loneliness, a terrible rejection. That's a much greater hunger."[15]

Mother Teresa concludes that the unfulfilled need for love and feelings of rejection and loneliness are a far greater suffering than starvation and poverty. I find it very difficult to decide which is the more urgent human need, to be loved or to be fed. Poverty, malnutrition, and illness are just as disastrous to the human spirit as rejection and lovelessness. In actuality, many people are subjected to both extremes. For example, the Untouchables and the destitutes in the slums of India are not only impoverished and malnourished but they are also isolated and rejected by society.

Many religious organizations and churches in the United States are striving to solve the problems of isolation, loneliness, drug abuse and alcoholism in their communities by providing food, medical care, financial assistance, and most importantly, spiritual counseling to the needy. In addition, numerous social and government agencies offer aid to the poor, the handicapped, the sick and the elderly. In India too, the government is committed to tackling the social problems through a variety of programs. Mother Teresa has elaborated that "the government of India has many fine programs . . . and we have excellent relations with the government. They have given me a free pass on the national Indian Airline. The government is trying to do many things, but we are working among the poorest of the poor. That is the work we have chosen to do."[16]

As a dedicated servant of Christ, Mother Teresa speaks with direct simplicity on basic human issues of the value and meaning of human existence, reaching the hearts and minds of her listeners. She expresses her beliefs on human responsibility with unflinching voice and spreads Christ's message wherever she has been invited to speak or to open a service center. When Mother Teresa addresses a gathering, she exudes a glowing spiritual charisma which touches each individual as if she is talking to each one personally. For her, Jesus' message is clear and unequivocal and she joyfully spreads the good news of Christianity. "You are the light of the world. A city on a hill cannot be hidden. Neither do people light a lamp and put it under a bowl. Instead they put it on its stand, and it gives light to everyone in the house. In the same way, let your light shine before men, that they may see your good deeds and praise your Father in heaven." (Matthew 5:14-16)

Mother Teresa's basic philosophy is one of responding to the human need, hour by hour, day by day, whether the need is for food, for love, for prayer, or for medicine. She firmly believes that the problems of each society can be solved. The individual is the starting point and the willingness to unselfishly do little things for good must be in our hearts and minds so that creative cooperation and sharing can come about. The individual should first extend concern and help to the

immediate family, then to neighbors and neighbor-
hoods, and gradually the spirit of loving cooperation and concern will expand to communities
and even to the wider realm of states and nations.
Mother Teresa's life is proof of the power and
success of caring and sharing on a person-to-person
basis. Her desire to respond to the needs of destitute individuals led to the establishment of the
Missionaries of Charity and, as their members grew,
missionary centers spread throughout India and
around the world. Mother Teresa's words, "let us
try to find the poor, first in our family, in our
communities,"[17] refer particularly to those who
long for human relationships and long to be respected and recognized as persons with dignity.
Mother Teresa understands the frailty of human
nature in carrying out good intentions. "It is
easy to love people who are giving to me" but the
real love emerges when we can give love without
expecting anything in return because the very act
of loving is in itself a reward. "Come to know
your poor . . . If you know them, you will love
them. And if you love them, you will help them.
Let us begin our love at home."[18]

At times, our conscience tells us the right
thing to do but, with full awareness, we shirk from
loving or helping another because love often
demands sacrifice, sometimes great sacrifice. If
we want to avoid sacrifice, we cannot love freely
or give freely. Utilitarian calculations have no
place in love. Quoting from her personal experience, Mother Teresa narrates: "I will never forget
how a little Hindu child of four years taught me
how to love with great love. It was a time in
Calcutta when we had no sugar, and I do not know
how that little one heard 'Mother Teresa has no
sugar for her children.' He went home to his
parents and told them, 'I will not eat sugar for
three days, I'll give my sugar to Mother Teresa.'

That little one loved with great love. He loved until it hurt."[19]   While giving a speech in Fort Wayne, Indiana, Mother Teresa told of how a paralyzed man living in the U.S., who had the use of only one arm and hand, sacrificed two weeks money which he would have spent on cigarettes, and gave it to her for the poor.   "It is not how much we do, but how much love we put into the doing."[20]

Just before leaving Fort Wayne Indiana, after addressing a packed audience, Mother Teresa received a request that she write a little note to a girl who was terminally ill from a rare blood disease and bedridden in a Lutheran hospital in the city.   In spite of her busy schedule, Mother Teresa made time to stop at the hospital on her way to the airport to visit Molly Offerly and her parents.   By the time Mother Teresa arrived, Molly was in a deep coma.   Mother Teresa and Molly's parents prayed together and, the next morning, the little girl died.

Mother Teresa narrates another beautiful personal experience:

"I never forget," she said, reiterating the story of a man she saw on the streets of London some years ago.   "He was so lonely, so poor. I shook his hand--my hand is always so warm--and he looked at me and said it had been so long since he had felt the warmth of a human hand and that he knew I was someone who really cared about him."

"I never realized before that such a small action could bring so much happiness."[21]

Mother Teresa has delivered the message of love
over and over again. Is this the saintly quality
we find in her? Is she really a living saint? She
replies to the question by saying: "Possibly they
see Jesus in me. Holiness is not extraordinary.
It is in you. It is in everybody. Close contact
with the Eucharist and with the poor is the quick-
est way to holiness--if we have Jesus in our
hearts."[22]

Mother Teresa sees a close bond between love,
prayer, and faith. "If all of us spent a little
more time on our knees in prayer to God, we would
then begin to love. If you love, you cannot hurt
anyone." And again:

> The fruit of faith is always love.
> The fruit of love is action. We
> must put our love for Jesus in a living
> action.
> How do we do that?
> If we do it with Jesus, if we do it
> for Jesus, and if we do it to Jesus,
> then we know that we are with Him
> because He has said so . . . "I was
> hungry, you gave Me to eat; I was
> naked, and you clothed Me...
> And to be able to do that, we need
> the Eucharist, we need Jesus in the
> Holy Communion, we need the Bread of
> Life.
> That's why Jesus made Himself the
> Bread of Life to satisfy our hunger for
> His Love . . .
> Then He makes Himself the Hungry
> One so that we can satisfy His hunger
> for our love.[23]

If we fail to love, if we do not care for our
fellow human beings, we will be held accountable to
God for our failures because "at the hour of our

death, all of us are going to be judged on one point—what we have been to each other and how we have done to the least among us. Homelessness, can be homelessness of being rejected, unwanted, unloved. Hunger can be the hunger of simply wanting to be somebody."[24]

Mother Teresa is a living legend of dedicated action and singleminded determination. I was told by Sister Vida of the Missionaries of Charity, that Mother Teresa works very hard and sleeps only for a few hours per night. In addition to Mother's daily work with the needy, she, as the Superior General of the Missionaries of Charity, makes most of the administrative and organizational decisions for the Order. Her activities depend upon the need of the hour. When a group of journalists clamored for an interview at the New Delhi airport in 1979, Mother Teresa told them: "We are bound to the unwanted, the poor, the hungry and the naked. If I find one hungry for bread or love, I feed."[25]

A news reporter asked Mother Teresa at a press conference, "Do your nuns ever suffer from 'burnout'?". Mother Teresa couldn't understand the term, "burnout," as it does not exist in her dictionary or her experience. After hearing the explanation of the word, she replied that her sisters do not suffer burnout because the poor "give us so much more than we give them."[26]

Much of Mother Teresa's practical success in uplifting the poor lies in the fact that she has always insisted that those whom she assists be actively engaged in work, such as handicrafts, carpentry, agriculture, cobblery, housing construction, making paper bags to be sold to the shops, etc. Whatever the task, she rightly believes that work instills self-confidence, dignity and purpose to life. After I visited Mother Teresa in Calcutta, many of my friends in India, as well as in California, asked me about her "secret for success" because people are very much intrigued by her personality. I believe that she holds no special secret for success. Rather, her whole life has followed the teachings of Christ in practicing love, prayer, sacrifice and hard work. As T. S. Eliot said: "We know too much, and are convinced of too little."[27] That is why we look for secret new recipes for success and happiness instead of following the simple truths which have been proven successful through the generations.

In addition to Mother Teresa's teachings on love, sacrifice, prayer and work, there is another important point which she tirelessly stresses on every possible occasion, namely her opposition to abortion. In her Nobel Prize acceptance speech, given before King Olav and invited guests in Norway in 1979, Mother Teresa said: "To me the nations who have legalized abortion are the poorest nations. They are afraid of the unborn child and the child must die."[28] Mother Teresa called on the king and the audience to pray and stand by the unborn child. She believes that abortion is the cause of evil and suffering in the world. She told a gathering of women in New Delhi in 1979: "If a mother can destroy her child then how can you stop people from killing one another . . . In all the suffering we see I ask myself why. The answer is that we are destroying the child. The life God has created, we kill . . . We have been created to love. I beg you to use that power."[29]

While at Marquette University, Mother Teresa again spoke forcefully on the issue:

> And today, no one is more unwanted, no one is more unloved than the little unborn child. And yet, we know it was

the little unborn child that recognized
the presence of Christ when Mary came
to Elizabeth. The little one in the
womb of Elizabeth leaped with joy at
the presence of Christ. And today, let
us all unite to pray that in this our
beautiful country, we will make sure
that we want the child; that we will go
with Mary in search, and that we will
not allow a single child, a single
unborn child, to feel unwanted, unloved, uncared for. For me, abortion
is the greatest poverty that the nation
can have, can experience.[30]

Mother Teresa does not simply criticize abortion but offers an alternative solution. "I'm
fighting abortion by adoption. Destroying an
innocent child is the greatest sin. If a mother
can kill her own innocent child, then no one is
safe."[31] Referring to abortion as America's
"poverty of spirit," she had boldly told the U.S.
audience: "If you don't want that little child,
that unborn child, give him to me. I want him."[32]
Her condemnation of abortion gives strong support
to "pro-life" groups in the United States, since
the question of abortion is both a religious and
political issue. However, Mother Teresa's views on
this matter are based solely on her religious
beliefs. According to Edward Le Joly, Mother
Teresa's spiritual advisor, "Pope John Paul II has
personally asked Mother . . . to preach against
abortion everywhere in the world. She and the Holy
Father are very much alike in their faith."[33]

After Mother Teresa was awarded the Nobel Peace
prize, public recognition of her name and her work
has increased tremendously around the world. As a
result, she has had many opportunities to speak on
the subject of abortion. Nevertheless, her stance

on abortion has been consistent even from the early days of her work in Calcutta. After establishing Shishu Bhavan (Children's Home), Mother Teresa personally appealed to women at the abortion clinics in Calcutta to forgo abortion and give her their babies for adoption.

Mother Teresa has critics in spite of all the good which she and the Missionaries of Charity are doing. Some people think that the western mass media have promoted Mother Teresa as a popular religious hero while ignoring many other missionaries who have worked silently with the same spiritual dedication. Mother Teresa doesn't enjoy the publicity and demands placed upon her and she does not seek out speaking engagements and public ceremonies. Rather, she considers any invitations which she receives as the will of Jesus. For instance, when Mother Teresa accepted the invitation to receive the Pere Marquette Discovery Award at Marquette University, she commented: "I do not know why Jesus does things like this." Again, while in San Francisco, she stressed: "It is a big sacrifice for me to travel . . . and I keep praying 'please give me the freedom so I don't have to go.' I miss my Sisters very much. I need the Sisters and the Sisters need me. But I use the opportunity to travel to tell people about the great needs of the poor for love."[34]

Dick Ryan, a columnist for the New York Daily News, wrote a critical analysis in the National Catholic Reporter on Mother Teresa's popularity in the United States. Among other topics, he raised a very important issue. "Outside of abortion, Mother Teresa has never used her high visibility to attack some of the underlying causes of problems around the world that are so punishing to the poor, women, minorities, the imprisoned, the disenfranchised."[35]

There is no doubt that Mother Teresa is a powerful popular figure but she seldom gets entangled with political and social issues. As an Indian citizen who has lived and worked in Calcutta for over a half century, Mother Teresa has a tremendous influence and insight into India's social problems. If she would have spoken publicly on the social and political issues in India, her words would have exerted a very strong positive force. But, she would also have become a part of the confrontations between political factions and politicians would have used her name to support their respective parties in their struggle for power. Such controversies would have jeopardized Mother Teresa's whole life's mission of working for the poorest of the poor. She has been able to co-exist with many different religious and political organizations without taking sides and, thereby, she has won the admiration and respect of one and all. Because of Mother Teresa's neutrality in these matters, even the Marxist government of Calcutta holds her in high esteem.

In August 1982, Pope John Paul II asked Mother Teresa to go to war-torn Lebanon as his emissary of peace. To date, this is the first time Mother Teresa has become involved in a political confrontation. Pope John Paul II sent Mother Teresa as his emissary because she "already knows the language of peace, without having studied many manuals, because this [language] belongs to Christian formation, to Christian spirituality, to her soul, to her genius, to her heart." Mother Teresa sorrowfully commented upon the situation in Beirut: "I have never been in a war before, but I have seen famine and death. I was asking myself, 'What do they feel when they do this?' I don't understand it. They are all the children of God. Why do they do it?"

32

Mother Teresa is not a social and political reformer although her speeches on love, family, neighbors, service and charity contain social and religious ideals which are the cornerstone of society. As a devout nun, she has given abundantly to this world through her exemplary life of faith, devotion, poverty, sacrifice, and service. In recognition of her great spiritual service, Mother Teresa has been given numerous prizes, cash awards and honors. Apart from the Nobel Prize for Peace, the Magsaysay Award was presented to her by the Phillipine government, the Pope John XXIII Peace Prize in Rome, the Jawaharlal Nehru Award, the Joseph Kennedy Jr. Foundation Award, the Padma Shree and the highest honor of the Bharat Ratna (Jewel of India) were awarded by the Indian government, the Pere Marquette Discovery Award, and scores of honorary doctorates from internationally famous universities.

In the words of Reverend John P. Raynor, the President of Marquette University:

> How blessed we are and how privileged, today, to hear in the word of God, and to see in her life our basic call and inspiration, individually and personally, each in our own way,
> --to seek God in all persons and in all things,
> --to radiate, in all we do, our faith and our hope and our love of God,
> --and to share the riches of the divine life which have been given to us freely and undeservedly to share them with others so that we can, with Mother Teresa, bend every effort to bring people closer to God, for His Greater Honor and Glory.[36]

PRAYER, POVERTY AND SERVICE

The life of the Missionaries of Charity can be succinctly summed up in three keywords: prayer, poverty, and service.

PRAYER

Prayer and devotion play a primary role in the daily living of the Missionaries of Charity. A typical day starts with the celebration of Holy Mass, communion, meditation and prayer. The sisters leave at 7:30 in the morning for their assigned areas of service. Their busy daily schedule also includes prayer before lunch and an hour of adoration in the evening before supper. According to one sister in Calcutta, "without prayer, we cannot do the kind of work we are doing." The Missionaries of Charity draw their strength and stamina from daily spiritual renewal. A life of total surrender to the will of Jesus Christ and the imitation of His life and teachings are their hallmark.

I witnessed cases of horrendous leprosy in Calcutta, wherein people are afraid to touch or even look at the leprosy victim. The sisters and brothers have no fear. They clean and bandage the studded hands and feet, clean the open, oozing sores, and give abundantly of Christ's love to these suffering people. It is the indomitable faith and trust they have in Jesus which gives them the courage and gladness to serve. This special kind of service is possible only in and through faith.

Mother Teresa considers it a great gift to be able to serve Jesus through the poor. The sisters give selflessly of love and service to the poor and expect nothing in return. Rather, the very act of giving in love is its own reward. As Mother Teresa has often said, the poor "give us so much more than we give them." The Missionaries of Charity's dedication to following the will of Jesus is the secret of their lifetime service. They do not count on material success symbols, such as buildings or bank accounts, to boast how greatly the Lord has blessed them.

If one wants to help the destitute out of pity, desire for social justice, or for any other reason, one can do it with determination for a limited period of time. But seldom can one make a commitment for one's whole life. When I lived in Vancouver, Canada, I worked as a volunteer at Saint James Social Service which is run by Mrs. May Gutteridge, who has been doing Christian service similar to that of the Missionaries of Charity on a small scale for many years. Saint James Social Service caters to the needs of alcoholics, drug addicts, the poor, and shut-ins. As a philosopher, I wanted to gain a better understanding of these societal problems and much to my surprise, I found that counseling and listening to serious problems day after day was an exhausting experience. I was shocked to find that even some successful, educated professional people had ruined their lives and ended up in the slums due to alcohol and drug abuse and alienation from their families and society. The most frustrating and depressing experience for me was the fact that, in spite of counsel and encouragement, most of those who came to the center lacked the will to struggle with their problems and had simply given up.

Some people work in the slums with the intention of improving the economic and social conditions of the destitute, often with the expectation that they will see measurable improvements within a set time span. Although many poor individuals are greatly aided by the humanitarian assistance of social workers and volunteers, there never seems to be an end to the problems and suffering of people. Without the strength and grace found in spirituality, it is easy to become disillisioned, frustrated and bitter about the terrible lot of the impoverished.

I asked Mother Teresa how is it possible to have unshakable faith in God all the time and serve Him singlemindedly. She replied with a graceful smile: "Just as we need food to nourish our body, we need Holy Communion to strengthen our spirit. The more regularly we receive it, the more strength we get." While in San Francisco, Mother Teresa reaffirmed the importance of Holy Communion. "I need the Eucharist. My life is interwoven with the Eucharist. We do not do just social work--we are contemplative Sisters working among the poorest of the poor."[1] A prayer card sent to me by the Missionaries of Charity beautifully sums up the idea: "Jesus has given Himself to us in the Eucharist to satisfy our hunger, and He gives Himself to us in the poor so that we might satisfy His hunger."

Normally when we pray, we ask God for gifts, personal favors and material prosperity. But prayer does not operate in the sense of the economic theory of supply and demand. Rather, prayer is a total surrender to God and a striving to carry out His will as He directs us. "Thy will be done."

It is an unconditional, cheerful attitude of "let go!" We need to strengthen our faith in and through prayer, as it is the only direct link of communication with God. This channel is open to everyone but we don't often use it in the right spirit.

Sometimes, we encounter people who are disappointed that their prayers have not been answered and events in their life did not turn out the way in which they had anticipated. As a result of such experiences, a person may become cynical and bitter about prayer itself. We should not think that we can get all of our wishes fulfilled just because we pray. Prayer is an internal spiritual experience and a means of increasing our spiritual stamina to meet the challenges of life. God's plan for our lives may be far different from what we expect it to be. A genuine prayer for a genuine need will often be answered. Otherwise, "when you ask, you do not receive, because you ask with wrong motives, that you may spend what you get on your pleasures." (James 4:3)

Whatever the brothers and sisters of the Missionaries of Charity do, Jesus and prayer are in their minds and hearts. When they walk in the slums or travel in railroad trams, they silently pray the rosary. The sisters and brothers have served as a guiding light to many people by their simple, holy lifestyle. For more than three decades, they have served the poor without publicity, quietly, on a person-to-person basis.

After Mother Teresa accepted the Nobel Peace Prize, people began to look up to her as a VIP who has been endowed with spiritual enlightenment and who is carrying on a special mission with her unique gifts. Even though she has been called a "living saint," Mother Teresa, in all humility,

points out clearly that no one should look up to
her, but only to Jesus, as poetically expressed in
the prayercard, "Radiating God's Love," which was
sent to me by the Missionaries of Charity:

Dear Jesus help me to spread Thy
fragrance everywhere I go. Flood my
soul with Thy spirit and life.

Penetrate and possess my whole being
so utterly that all my life may only be
a radiance of Thine.

Shine through me, and be so in me
that every soul I come in contact with
may feel Thy presence in my soul.

Let them look up and see no longer
me—but only Jesus! Stay with me then I
shall begin to shine as Thou dost; so to
shine as to be a light to others.

The light O Jesus will be all from
Thee; none of it will be mine; it will
be Thou shining on others through me.

Let me thus praise Thee in the way
Thou dost love best, by shining on those
around me.

Let me preach Thee without preaching, not by words but by my example, by
the catching force, the sympathetic
influence of what I do, the evident
fulness of the love my heart bears to
Thee. Amen.

POVERTY

There are two common paths traveled in God's
service. The first path is to work hard, gain
material prosperity, and then share one's wealth
with those who are less fortunate. The second path
is to sacrifice oneself and one's possessions in
the action of service. A person may renounce even

the ordinary comforts of life in total dedication and sacrifice. These two paths have been clearly recognized by most Christian denominations and both ways of life can lead to spiritual fulfillment.

The voluntary acceptance of strict poverty is the second characteristic of the Missionaries of Charity. When Mother Teresa left the Loretto school and convent, her vision was to share the life of the poorest of the poor and to minister to their needs. The Missionaries of Charity have scant material possessions. Each sister has two simple white sarees, a piece of soap, a bucket, and a straw mat. She is ready to serve! Even in the sweltering heat and humidity of Calcutta, the sisters have no fans in their convent. The spartan way of life of the Missionaries of Charity reminds me of the life of poverty voluntarily chosen by Mahatma Gandhi. He also had no possessions of any worth and led a life dedicated to serving the Indian outcastes and Untouchables. In the traditional Hindu, Buddhist, and Jaina religions, non-possession (A-parigraha) is the first prerequisite for entering the spiritual life.

Poverty is a God-given spiritual dowry for the Missionaries of Charity. Their life is extremely austere by our worldly standards. They depend entirely upon donations to feed the hungry. The sisters' daily food is the same as that served to the destitute. They neither store food reserves nor concern themselves with how it will be provided. As Jesus said: "Do not worry about your life, what you will eat or drink; or about your body, what you will wear. Is not life more important than food, and the body more important than clothes? Look at the birds of the air; they do not sow or reap or store away in barns, and yet your heavenly Father feeds them. Are you not much more valuable than they?" (Matthew 6:25,26) In Mother

Teresa's words, "God is our Banker, He always provides." The expansion of their Order in India and around the world is, in itself, a clear testimony that the invisible hand of God has guided them.

When Mother Teresa agreed to open a mission in downtown Miami, Florida, to serve destitute women who are mostly drug addicts and prostitutes, Monsignor Bryan O. Walsh, Director of the Catholic Charities of the Archdiocese of Miami, said that the sisters requested their quarters include no refrigerators or air-conditioning. "They don't keep food in the house overnight," said Walsh, "Simplicity is the word!"

"Poverty is freedom" according to Mother Teresa. Only those who have renounced all material goods or those who do not have attachment to their possessions will be able to appreciate and understand this idea. People have criticized Mother Teresa for idealizing poverty, just as Mahatma Gandhi did, because the glorification of poverty does nothing to aid society in combating the problems. This criticism is totally unjustified. Mother Teresa is not preaching poverty but working to uplift the poorest of the poor. She and her sisters have taken the vow of poverty as a spiritual discipline, in imitation of the life of Jesus Christ. If there were no suffering destitutes in Calcutta, I am sure that Mother Teresa would be the first to rejoice. "Poverty is freedom" implies that, as long as our minds and hearts are set only in pursuit of material riches, our spirit cannot be free.

Much misery today stems from selfish greed. We can spend our whole lives, consciously or unconsciously, pursuing material security. The quest for material security as an end in itself slowly and silently dries up our innate spiritual and creative potential. Man is primarily a spiritual being but this aspect of our existence is often deliberately ignored. Even if we channel our intelligence, energy, knowledge, and opportunities to gain material prosperity, we should not forget that lasting satisfaction lies in realizing our spiritual potential and in contributing to make this world a better place to live. Sharing and caring is a true sign of spirituality.

The uniqueness of the vows of the Missionaries of Charity lies not in the fact that they have renounced the material world but that they also practice spirituality in action by being concretely involved in alleviating the suffering of others. To use the terminology of the Bhagavad Gita, the Missionaries of Charity are "karma yogis" (yogis of action).[2]

The vow of poverty taken by the sisters and brothers parallels the Hindu ideal of renunciation of the material world to see the world of the spirit. Indian yogis have traditionally become recluses to seek the heights of spiritual experience through meditation. A few of the recluses then return to society to give discourses on their spiritual experiences and to share the wisdom gained from their reflections. However, most yogis are only interested in seeking personal salvation. Ever since the benefits of yoga for physical health and mental tranquility have been popularized in the U.S. and Europe, Westerners have become far more interested in the practice of yoga than Indians themselves. In fact, knowledgeable yogis in India usually want to come to the western countries and establish their religious empires. Unfortunately, in present day India, genuine yogis are hard to find and there are relatively few centers for the study of yoga when compared to the size of the population.

I mentioned to Mother Teresa that, in spite of the prosperity in the western world, so many people are not happy. By contrast, I see that the sisters in Calcutta are so content and cheerful, radiating love, gladness, and joy. What is the secret of this happiness? Her reply was straightforward: "We don't have any possessions, therefore, we don't worry about anything. So, we are happy."

SERVICE

Prayer and poverty culminate in concrete action for the Missionaries of Charity. Prayer is action and action is prayer. Prayer without action is blind and action without prayer is directionless. As the Bhagavad Gita says, seek "immortality in action." The Missionaries of Charity see Jesus incarnated in their active service. Simply put, they do all for Jesus, following Christ's own teachings because action is the core of Christian responsibility.

> For I was hungry and you gave me food,
> I was thirsty, and you gave me drink,
> I was a stranger and you welcomed me.
> I was naked and you clothed me,
> I was sick and you visited me,
> I was in prison and you came to me.
>   (Matthew 25:35,36, RSV)

At times, Jesus' words, "you will always have the poor with you," have been misinterpreted to imply a predestined fatalism, i.e., poverty and discrimination are sanctioned by Divine Providence. But, Jesus also emphatically pointed out that "whatever you did not do for one of the least of these, you did not do for me." (Matthew 25:45)

Peace and prosperity are possible for any society only when people recognize the unfortunate plight of the poor and help them to help themselves. Giving and sharing is a spiritual act which establishes the mutual brotherhood between man and man. "If anyone has material possessions and sees his brother in need but has no pity on him, how can the love of God be in him? Dear children, let us not love with words or tongue but with actions and in truth." (I John 3:17,18)

Mother Teresa has always recognized the fact that it is not enough to feed the hungry, heal and comfort the sick, and provide shelter for the homeless. Those in need also need guidance to live a productive and dignified life. The sisters and brothers take a pragmatic approach in aiding the poor, using imagination and organizational skills. They have taught lepers the art of weaving clothes and other handicrafts. Whenever houses are constructed for the poor, garden plots are planned to grow vegetables and grain. The sisters teach people how to make ropes from coconut shells and paper bags from discarded newspapers, which can then be sold. Abandoned children are given hope for a better future through adoption into families in India and abroad. These are just a few instances which exemplify the Missionaries of Charity's creative guidance in helping the poorest of the poor to help themselves.

No opportunity is missed by Mother Teresa to put her resources skillfully to the service of the poor. When Pope Paul VI visited India, he donated his Lincoln Continental to Mother Teresa. She set up a lottery raffle and raised much more money than the car was worth. When Mother Teresa went to Oslo, Norway, to accept the Nobel Prize, she declined the traditional dinner party, which cost about 30,000 Norwegian crowns ($6,000). She asked the Nobel Committee to drop the dinner and donate the money which would feed about four hundred poor people in Calcutta for one year. The committee gladly complied with her request and held a simple reception in place of the dinner. Mother Teresa said that she would use the Nobel Prize cash award to "build more homes for the destitute and the poor, especially lepers." Again, when Mother Teresa went to Washington, D.C. to receive the 1982 Brien McMahon Memorial Award, which is usually presented at a special dinner hosted by the Fordham University Club of Washigton, D.C., Mother Teresa requested that the dinner be cancelled and the money be donted to help the poor. The Fordham University Club agreed to her request.

Let me again emphasize that the service of the Missionaries of Charity is not simply catering to the physical needs of the poorest of the poor, but something much more significant. Their service is a genuine response, recognizing each individual with dignity and respect. This is the core of Christian love. "For anyone who does not love his brother, whom he has seen, cannot love God, whom he has not seen." (I John 4:20) Mother Teresa has reflected that "in these years of work among the people, I have come more and more to realize that it is being unwanted that is the worst disease that any human being can experience."[3]

Why do we neglect and ignore our fellow human beings? It seems that we become so involved with our day-to-day business and our concern for self-advancement that we lose sight of the problems of others and we often fail in individual moral commitment and responsibility toward our fellow man. Each small act of kindness and love, however insignificant it may seem, contributes to the well-being of society as a whole. Whenever greed and selfishness take priority in human actions, the society stagnates. Gandhi has put it very aptly:

"The earth provides for every man's need but not for every man's greed." Mother Teresa shares Gandhi's view: "Greed . . . is the greatest obstacle to peace in the world today--greed for power, for money and for name."[4]

According to Mother Teresa, "we need to tell the poor that they are somebody to us, that they have been created with the same loving hand of God, to love and be loved."[5] She has pointed out again and again that we should serve and love our family first, then our neighbors, and then society. This is a beautiful concept which everyone can practice. No one in this universe is useless. Each has something special to offer in thoughts, words and deeds. We need to reflect upon the gifts which we possess and how to best use these gifts. "There are different kinds of spiritual gifts, but the same Spirit. There are different kinds of service, but the same Lord. There are different kinds of working, but the same God works all of them in all men." (I Corinthians 12:4-6)

Love in action is the philosophy of life of the Missionaries of Charity. In Mother Teresa's words, "realize that love means actions . . . It is the most important thing. If people will serve the poor they will always continue to love."[6] Mahatma Gandhi once said: "In my judgement, the Christian faith does not lend itself to much preaching or talking. It is best propagated by living it . . . When will you Christians really crown Jesus as the prince of peace and proclaim through your deeds as the champions of the poor and the oppressed?"[7] If Gandhi were alive today, he would have been over-whelmed by the actions of the Missionaries of Charity and by the abundance of their love.

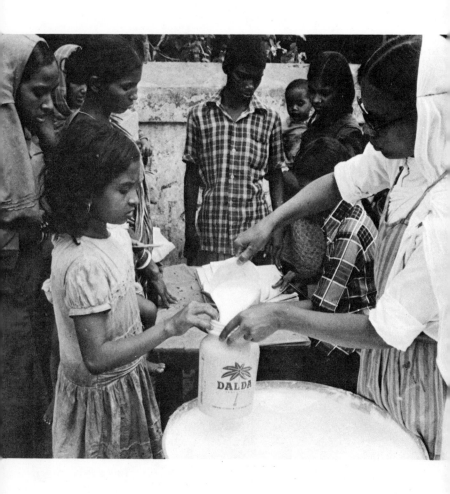

SHISHU BHAVAN

According to the Gospel of Luke, one day the disciples were arguing among themselves as to which of them was the greatest. "When Jesus perceived the thought of their hearts, he took a child and put him by his side, and said to them, 'Whoever receives this child in my name receives me, and whoever receives me receives him who sent me; for he who is least among you all is the one who is great.'" (Luke 9:47,48 RSV) The Gospel of Mark also narrates Jesus' great love for children. "Whoever receives one such child in my name receives me; and whoever receives me, receives not me but him who sent me." (Mark 9:37, RSV)

To quote Mother Teresa, "loving the child is the most important thing . . . It is much more important than riches."[1] Shishu Bhavan, located not far from the mother house in Calcutta, offers loving care, shelter and hope for abandoned babies and orphaned children. This center also provides other necessary services for the poor in addition to caring for children. There is a small kitchen adjacent to the courtyard where food is cooked and distributed to the poor every day. Each morning, a long line of hungry people wait to enter through a small gate into the courtyard of Shishu Bhavan to receive food. This may be their only meal for the day. Next to the courtyard is a small office where the poor come to explain their problems and ask for counseling and for financial help. The sisters also distribute medications to the sick and give basic first aid.

While I was waiting to see Sister Agnes, who is the main administrator of Shishu Bhavan, I noticed a sickly woman in a wheelchair, probably in her late twenties, who was writing something very neatly in English. When I talked to her, I was amazed by her style and fluency in English coupled with a fine sense of humor. This lady must have had a good university education. Due to tuberculosis and an auto accident, she had spent all of her money on medical care, was paralyzed from the waist down, and could not work. She had come to Shishu Bhavan to ask Sister Agnes for help. There are no welfare programs in India like in the western countries and, if a person is unable to work, he or she must depend entirely upon the family or receive some aid from charitable institutions. Many end up totally destitute in the ghettos.

I met briefly with Sister Agnes who was extremely busy attending to the needs of the poor. She is very calm and polite and her conversation is succinct. Sister Agnes asked Sister Hyacinth to show me around and explain their work. There are two wings in Shishu Bhavan, one for the care of abandoned infants, and the other for temporarily nursing ill and malnourished babies. Since poor parents cannot provide adequate nourishment and medical care for their infants, they bring them to Shishu Bhavan when they fall sick. The sisters care for them until they are healthy and strong enough to return home to their families.

Unwed pregnant women who are homeless and do not want to keep their babies are encouraged to stay at Shishu Bhavan until their delivery. The Missionaries of Charity will gladly accept and care

for the newborn infants and find families to adopt
them. It is heartbreaking to see how mothers can
mercilessly discard their newborn infants; but, at
the same time, it is a joy to see that the babies
at Shishu Bhavan have been fortunate to have found
a safe and loving haven, while many abandoned
infants never see the light of day. As we were
walking through the rows of cradles, Sister
Hyacinth commented, pointing to a two-day old baby,
that he was found in the street by the police that
very morning. The baby had a deformed nose and a
mangled upper lip. Most abandoned babies are found
near refuse dumps, in the gutters, or in front of
churches and police stations.

Some of the tiny infants were sleeping serenely
like angels. Quite a few were being drip-fed
intravenously. Some had severe breathing problems.
Often babies are born prematurely in the slums
either due to the malnutrition of the mother or
because the mother is a prostitute who has tried
all kinds of local drugs to abort the pregnancy.
Many of the premature infants die within hours or
days of their birth. However, Shishu Bhavan gives
them a chance to survive. What I have described
here is my impression of the plight of these
innocent children. The whole tragic scene will,
naturally, leave one aghast and depressed. But for
the Missionaries of Charity, taking care of these
unwanted children is not a burden; rather, it is a
God-given privilege.

When I saw the deformed infants lying in their
cribs, I was reminded of a blind girl whom I had
seen at St. Catherine's Orphanage in Bombay a
number of years ago. I had gone to the orphanage,
incidentally, to visit a Belgian priest who was a
professor of philosophy in Poona and who was helping the sisters at St. Catherine's. He introduced
me to a very intelligent and talented blind girl.

When I asked the priest whether she was born blind, he sadly replied in the negative. He narrated that the parents of the girl had plucked out her eyes with the hope that people would pity her and she could survive as a beggar when she grew up. This girl was very fortunate to have been found by the nuns at the orphanage. After a few years, when I was studying in Germany, I was delighted to read in a newspaper that a German engineer had adopted this blind girl. The newspaper gave a short biography of her life. It is so beautiful and inspirational to hear of the good people do!

Whether the babies at Shishu Bhavan are healthy or sick, the sisters tenderly care for them with love and joy. As we walked by the rows of cradles, Sister Hyacinth pointed out individual infants, saying that this baby had been adopted by a French family, or an Indian family, or an Italian family. I told Sister Hyacinth how overwhelmed I was to see the love and affection that the sisters are pouring on these abandoned children. Sister Hyacinth replied with a smile: "Intellectually knowing and understanding love is not enough. One should have love from the heart."

A group of high school girls visited the center while I was there. The teacher undertook this creative educational venture to expose the girls to the realities of the life of the poor. From the private school uniform which the students wore, I gathered they they were all from middle and upper class families. As the students walked through the nursery, I saw the mixed emotions on their faces, happiness at the infants' sweet faces and shock at seeing those who were fed intravenously. I am sure that no amount of theoretical talk could re-place this first-hand experience. Such practical education about life will definitely have a power-ful influence on the students and will help them realize and remember their human responsibility and commitment toward helping those less fortunate.

One of Mother Teresa's main goals in establishing Shishu Bhavan has been to fight abortion through adoption. Her religious conviction is that "we have been created to love and not to kill." In India, religious people generally do not endorse abortion. Traditional Hindu religious belief emphatically affirms the sanctity of all life, both human and animal, and the value of nonviolence. Children are considered a precious gift from God.

The Missionaries of Charity run three main adoption centers in India, located in New Delhi, Bombay, and Calcutta. Sister Kalyani gave me detailed information about the procedures and regulations for adoption. Any family can adopt the babies but the sisters do not simply give the children away. They screen the applicants very carefully to determine the family's genuine interest and financial stability, so as to protect the children from becoming destitute again or becoming victims of child abuse. The prospective parents must have been married for five years and should be economically able to provide the basic necessities of life. The couple must show a firm commitment to child rearing and, every year, the parents must give a progress report to the Missionaries of Charity. Additionally, Mother Teresa is very strict on one point: ". . . I never give a child to a woman who has destroyed her own power of having a child."[2]

The sisters keep in touch with all their children in India and around the world. In June 1982, Mother Teresa said that she has stopped adoptions in the United States because so many families in India want to adopt the children. "There are many families in India who want these children--many of

them the offspring of unwed mothers—and all I ask
is that they love the child and give them a good
home."[3]

A lay worker was opening the day's mail at
Shishu Bhavan and smiled at the picture of a small
girl who lived with her adoptive parents in Italy.
As I was talking with Sister Kalyani, a couple with
a beautiful child walked in. The sisters came and
hugged the girl and talked with the family. The
father spoke proudly about his daughter's progress
in school. After they left, Sister Kalyani told me
that, years ago, this girl had been one of the
abandoned babies found in the street and brought to
Shishu Bhavan.

If so many thousands of street kids in India's
ghettos and in ghettos around the world would have
been given the opportunity to live in a home sur-
rounded by love, how they too would have bloomed
like the child I saw, developing their full potential and contributing positively to society. An
environment of love and nurture brings out the best
in all children and people often underestimate the
great human potential latent in the impoverished
youngsters. I was reminded of Elizabeth Browning's
poem, "The Cry of the Children:"

Do ye hear the children weeping, O my
brothers. . .?
. . . the young, young children, O my
brothers,
They are weeping bitterly!
They are weeping the playtime of the
others.[4]

When I visited Shishu Bhavan in April 1981, I
was told that there was a waiting list of 175
applicants to adopt a male child. Unfortunately,
boys are preferred over girls by Indian families

even in adoption. Some Indians even believe that bearing a female child is a sign of God's curse on them! Sons are considered an asset on pragmatic grounds because they are the wage earners and will support their parents in their old age. Having a son is a psychological consolation which gives the parents the feeling of existential security. On the contrary, having a female child is an economic burden. When a girl reaches marriageable age, the parents must negotiate and arrange her marriage and pay the full cost of the marriage ceremony and all related expenses. The groom's family is usually given gold jewelry, expensive sarees and dowry money. In addition, the bride's family serves a lavish lunch and dinner on the wedding day. In most cases, the poor and middle income families end up in debts which they must struggle to clear throughout their lifetime. Often, parents must pass on the marrige debts to their sons to pay off. If the parents cannot afford to marry their daughters, the girls must remain at home.

In the New Delhi area, there have been reports of newlywed women who were burned to death by their in-laws because the bride did not bring the promised dowry money with her. These murders have been dubbed as cooking accidents or suicides. The Indian government has passed laws prohibiting the practice of giving dowry but the laws are ignored most of the time. Unless there is a change in the mentality of the people, favoring fairness and justice toward women, the laws are futile. It is really tragic to see the plight of women from poor families in Indian society. They are the innocent victims of injustice and discrimination and the agony of existence is an everyday reality for many.

The cultural mental set and customary tradi-tions have trapped people into following the old ways even though many realize that it is morally unjust. If a family refuses to follow tradition, then arranging the marriages of their daughters will be very difficult and the family will often face isolation from the community and social embarrassment.

With the development of modern medical techniques, the bias against girl babies has taken a worse turn. Why should parents put up with the hardships of raising a female child when they can abort the pregnancy if the sex is determined to be female? Amniocentesis, the medical procedure which removes small amounts of amniotic fluid from a pregnant woman's uterus for examination, is usually performed to diagnose the existence of severe genetic disorders and birth defects in high-risk pregnancies. Incidentally, the sex of the fetus can also be determined by this test. Recently, there have been reports from New Delhi and Bombay that private medical clinics are offering amniocentesis solely to determine the sex of the fetus. If it is a female, the women are having an abortion. Women have been paying up to one hundred dollars to undergo the procedure, which is very costly by Indian standards. A few unscrupulous physicians are turning abortion into a profitable business enterprise by following the highly unethical practice of amniocentesis on demand.

If these doctors were really concerned about the welfare of their patients, they would never use amniocentesis indiscriminately. The women who go to these clinics are not aware of the fact that amniocentesis is risky both for them and for their unborn babies. A women can have internal hemorrhaging and even miscarriage after the procedure and the fetus may develop severe deformities, brain damage, or even death as a result of the test.

Mrs. Sushila Gopalan, a member of Parliament, has strongly spoken out against the sex bias in India: "In Uttar Pradesh, Bihar and Rajasthan, baby girls continue to be killed after birth . . . And now killing female fetuses has become big business."[5] The Indian Democratic Womens' Organization, feminists and other interested groups have been protesting the use of amniocentesis to determine sex.

Currently, amniocentesis is performed only in a few major cities in India. If aborting female fetuses becomes a popular and widespread practice in the society, thousands of amniocentesis clinics will crop up throughout the country in the next decade and the results will be disastrous. Since abortion has been legalized in India, the indiscriminate aborting of female fetuses poses a moral and legal dilemma for the government. Currently, there are approximately 935 females for every 1,000 males. This situation can lead to a severe population imblance between the sexes in the future.

Recently, the press has reported that mainland China is experiencing similar problems on a larger scale. Infanticide has dramatically increased in the rural areas of China, where approximately 800 million peasants live. Traditionally, male offspring have always been favored because they carry on the family name and inheritance, take care of their parents in their old age, and provide valuable labor in the fields. Since the Chinese government has adopted the policy of punishing couples who have more than one child, the killing of female infants after birth has risen markedly, in spite of the government's threat of stiff penalties.

The mother is held responsible for the sex of the baby she bears and the social pressures to deliver a baby boy are immense. There have been reports that outraged husbands have beaten both mother and baby, thrown them out of the house, and obtained a divorce after a female infant was born. Suffering rejection by both their husbands and family, many mothers are driven to suicide.

In China's cities, where amniocentesis and abortion are available, women pay large sums of money to determine the sex of the fetus and then have an abortion if it is a female. Chinese demographers have warned that dire consequences will result if nature's balance between males and females in the population is upset.

While I was visiting Shishu Bhavan in Calcutta, I saw an elderly, affluent, Hindu couple come in and talk to the sisters about the possibility of adopting a child. Later, when I was about to leave, I had a chance to talk with them. The couple were both very friendly and expressed how much joy Mother Teresa is giving to people like themselves, who are childless, by giving the opportunity to experience the pleasures and rewards of adoption. They said that they are well off economically but something important had been missing in their life, namely, a child of their own to love.

It is amazing to see how many thousands of children have found a safe home through Mother Teresa's program of adoption. Had not Mother Teresa and her sisters picked up the infants from the streets and gutters and had not Mother Teresa pleaded with expectant mothers to give the child to her rather than to have an abortion, thousands of children would not have been alive today. Mother Teresa has children all over the world, a great mother indeed!

During Mother Teresa's commencement address at
Harvard University in June 1982, a tender and
touching moment occurred when a dozen children, who
had been adopted by New England families, held up a
sign, "Hello Mother Teresa from your kids." They
all ran up to her at the podium and hugged her
joyously. One of the adopted children, Joffna
Johnston, reminisced on her life in Calcutta with
Mother Teresa: "She was always very calm. She took
care of me and never lost her temper."

Many cities in India have Shishu Bhavans.
Apart from Calcutta, I visited the Childrens' Homes
in Bangalore and Bombay. Bangalore is a clean and
beautiful city which enjoys a mild, temperate
climate and a standard of living far superior to
Calcutta. Although there are poor people in Bangalore, the city has no slums comparable to Calcutta.
Three sisters of the Missionaries of Charity are
working at the Shishu Bhavan which is located in a
quiet suburban neighborhood. There were approximately 45 babies and young children living at the
home and many of them were mentally and physically
handicapped. Some children were recouperating from
undernourishment and illness and would return to
their families after they regained their strength.
Sister Josephat, who is in charge of the center,
commented that "here in Bangalore the situation is
far better and Calcutta is a very hard case." In
addition to caring for children, the sisters have a
mobile clinic to treat people on the streets for
minor ailments. They also visit troubled families
to give counsel and assistance and offer spiritual
guidance. The sisters conduct sewing classes for
poor people who cannot afford to buy a sewing
machine so that they may find employment as
tailors.

In Bombay, there are two Shishu Bhavans. One
center is known as Asha Dan (Gift of Hope). The

building, donated by the Hindustan Lever Company, is situated at Sankley Street, Byculla. Sister Vida of the Missionaries of Charity talked with me about their work at Asha Dan. As we talked, she pointed out a group of mentally and physically handicapped children and said that "most of these children will remain in our care, as nobody wants to adopt them." Just as at the other centers run by the Missionaries of Charity, the sisters take care of abandoned babies and attend to destitutes who are terminally ill. I asked Sister Vida whether she feels any disgust or despair at times while doing this kind of work. She firmly replied, "We have grace from God to do the work."

Another Childrens' Home in Bombay is located at Ville Parle, in St. Francis Xavier Church Compound at Church Road. While I was there, Sister Doris pointed to all of the children who were playing in the yard, saying that "most of them have already been adopted and may leave soon." In response to my question, "What are your personal feelings about the service you are doing?", Sister Doris replied, "It is spiritual service we are doing but it should not be mistaken for social service and we are not social workers."

At each of the Missionaries of Charity's centers which I visited in India, I was deeply touched by their dedication and spirituality and the abundance of their faith and love. One question puzzled me all the time: How can a person develop such a great faith and love and is it really possible to live a life of faith and love each and every day? I asked Sister Kalyani about this in Calcutta. She said that the wavering of faith happens sometimes but we must go forward in faith and everything we do should proceed from faith. At times, we are selfish and we need to overcome our selfishness with love. Faith is a primary prerequisite do anything. Even scientists need faith that 1+1=2 before they prove it to be so. She continued that love must come from the heart and pointed to the importance of love in our life by quoting the words of St. Paul"

> If I speak in the tongues of men and of angels, but have not love, I am only a resounding gong or a clanging cymbal. If I have the gift of prophecy, and can fathom all mysteries and all knowledge, and if I have a faith that can move mountains, but have not love, I am nothing. If I give all I possess to the poor and surrender my body to the flames, but have not love, I gain nothing. (I Corinthians 13:1-3)

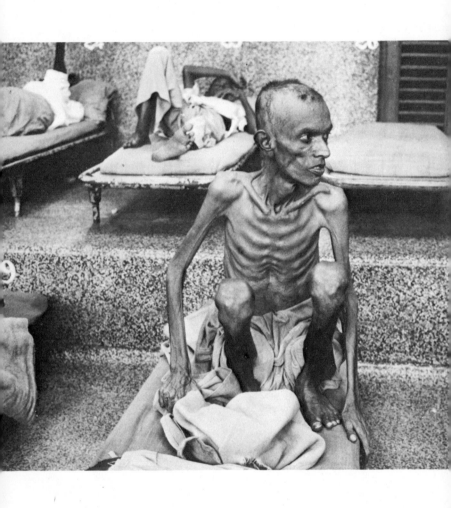

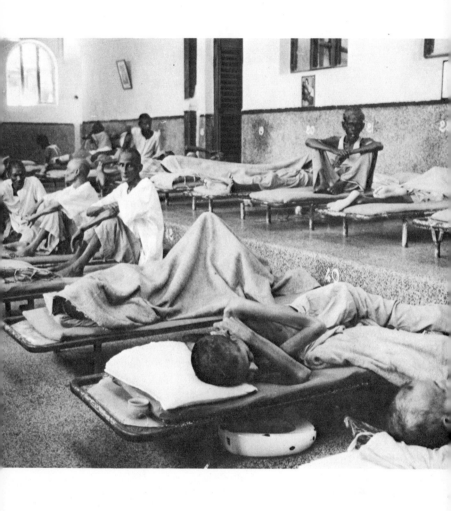

NIRMAL HRIDAY ·

On Sunday morning, after I met Mother Teresa and talked to her, I experienced inner joy and inspiration. Her utter simplicity, her holiness and, most of all, the serene flow of Jesus' message in her words had a powerful impact upon me. At the end of our conversation, I told Mother Teresa that I had not yet been to Nirmal Hriday. At once she replied: "Go to Kalighat and see our poor people. The Mass will be at 10:30 this morning."

On the previous day, I had debated within myself whether to go to Nirmal Hriday or not because, firstly, I had already seen so much concentrated misery in the slums during my stay in Calcutta and secondly, I was told by my friends in Calcutta that Nirmal Hriday is a very sorrowful place. When Mother Teresa said, "Go to Kalighat," my hestitation disappeared. My mind became serene and my emotions were elevated to a level of peaceful expectation coupled with prayerful thoughts to experience the spirituality of human existence with the dying at Nirmal Hriday.

Before reaching the Home for the Dying, while passing through the narrow, overcrowded lanes, I saw throngs of men and women with vermillion marks on their foreheads returning from the Hindu temple of the goddess Kali. I knew that Nirmal Hriday had been a guest house at one time for Hindu priests and pilgrims. The Corporation of Calcutta donated the kali Temple guest house to Mother Teresa so

that she could open a home for the dying destitutes. I asked someone in the crowd where Nirmal
Hriday was located, but even before he could reply,
a leper who was standing nearby enthusiastically
came forward and personally led me to Nirmal
Hriday.

In front of the main entrance is a plaque
enscribed:

Corporation of Calcutta
Nirmal Hriday
Home for Dying Destitutes

As I entered the passageway into the dimly lit
house, I saw rows of people lying on cots and
smelled peculiar odors. A poster was fastened on
the wall which read "Welcome to Mother's First
Love" and Mother Teresa's words: "Let every action
of mine be something beautiful for God." I stood
there silently in reflection and the thought
occurred to me that God has given a chance for some
of the dying destitutes to spend their last days of
earthly existence in dignity, being cared for as
persons. Nirmal Hriday is a living testimony and a
concrete expression of Christian love and responsibility. I read a beautiful prayer on the wall
which sums up the spirit and work of Mother Teresa
and her Missionaries of Charity:

Dear Lord, the great healer
I kneel before you
Since every good and perfect gift
Must come from you.
I pray, give skill to my hand
Clear vision to my mind
Kindness and sympathy to my heart
Give me the singleness of purpose,
Strength to lift at least a part of the

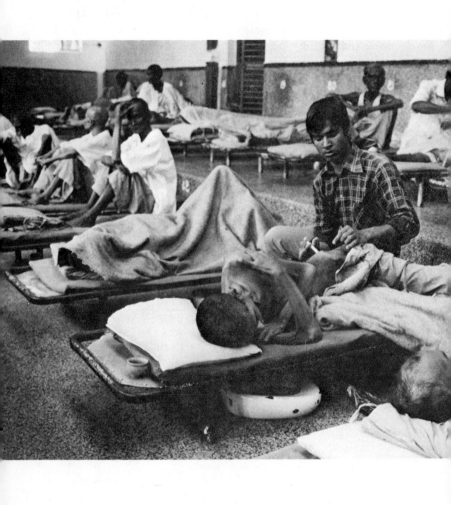

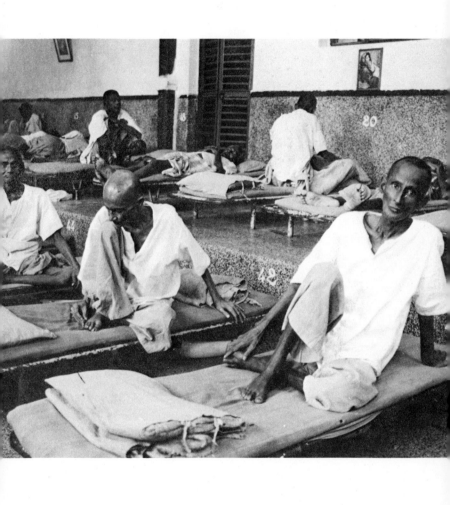

Burden of my suffering fellowmen,
And a true realization of the
Privilege that is mine.
Take from my heart all guile
And worldliness that with simple faith
Of a child I may rely on You.

There are two sections in Nirmal Hriday, each accommodating about sixty people, one for men and the other for women. A few people were crying loudly in agonizing pain and uttering "Mataji" or "Amma" (both mean "mother), their cries echoing intermittantly through the room. Some were just sitting on their cots very peacefully while others, who were unable to sit, were rolling from side to side in their beds, trying to find a comfortable position for their emaciated bodies to lie in rest. I saw a man sitting nearby who was the image of a living corpse. His protruding ribs could be counted even from a distance. I spoke to him but he couldn't respond. Breathing slowly, he looked at me with his sad eyes and that look expressed his state of being more powerfully than any words could. A young man carried in an extremely sick patient who was nothing but a bundle of bones enveloped in paper-thin skin, with torn patches on his back and shoulder blades exposing his bones. Later, the young man told me that he had given him a bath that morning and perhaps it was his last bath.

Finally, after having exprienced a hellish struggle for survival and being neglected, pitied, unloved and uncared for, these dying men and women have reached the final mile in their life's journey. At Nirmal Hriday, they find some relief from their struggles and can spend their final days or hours in dignity and peace. Mother Teresa speaks compassionately of the dying destitutes: "They never complain. They are going home to God and they don't struggle. We have picked up 42,000 people from the streets of Calcutta and 19,000 of them have died with us."[1] Mother Teresa tells of a moving and profound experience with a dying man at Nirmal Hriday. "I will never forget going down a street and I saw something moving in an open drain --it was a man in there. So, we picked him up and took him to the home and washed him and prepared him to die. He said. 'I have lived like an animal in the streets, but I am going to die like an angel.'"[2]

Ambulances and rickshaws bring terminally ill destitutes to Nirmal Hriday every day. However, those who come to this Home for the Dying need not be totally destitute. If the hospitals in Calcutta have no room to admit the poor people who are very sick, they are welcome at Nirmal Hriday. Some who are brought in even recover and are then able to resume their life.

Each person who comes to Nirmal Hriday is given personal care, respect and love. As soon as they arrive, the brothers or sisters bathe each one, often scraping off layers of accumulated filth and cleaning out maggot-infested wounds. The Missionaries of Charity even give holy water from the Ganges River to any Hindu who requests it. According to the popular Hindu belief, receiving holy water from the Ganges before death purifies one's soul and purges away one's sins. The brothers and sisters of the Missionaries of Charity give total attention and respect to each individual as a person with dignity. I asked Brother Stephen about the burial or cremation arrangements at Nirmal Hriday. He replied that voluntary organizations of Hindus, Moslems, and other religious groups bury or cremate the dead in accordance with their religious affiliation.

While I was at Nirmal Hriday, one of the brothers told me that a man was brought in an ambulance who was in horrible condition, with swollen, gangrenous legs and foul smells emanating from different parts of his body. The brother simply stated that he "cleaned and washed him and he is resting peacefully now." He also pointed out that "the persons who are lying on the lower side of the row are seriously sick and those who are lying on the upper level of the row are able to move and walk. Their chances of survival are better."

The sisters ask each one what they want to eat and what their needs are. One man, who had severe breathing problems and other medical complications, asked for rice, soup and a banana for lunch. The sister wrote down his request and said, "Is that all you want?" He nodded his head in total satisfation.

I also observed the lay workers shaving the men, giving head massages, and sitting beside the bed talking to each one. At times, the sick whispered to each other, sharing their sufferings and predicaments in life. Brother Shekar told me that "it is a joy to serve them because we also learn from them about life." One of the lay workers was sitting and holding the hand of a terminally ill man who was near death. A sister came over and told him not to sit with only one for a long time because others might think that he is going to die soon and, consequently, suffer fear and dread of their own death.

As we waited for the celebration of the Mass to begin, an altar was set up facing the people. Approximately twenty novices who are going to become sisters of the Missionaries of Charity had come to Nirmal Hriday to attend the Mass. Some men and women who were able to move about came forward to join in the service. The Mass, celebrated partly in English and partly in the Bengali language, was a most beautiful and spiritually moving experience. The terminally ill prayed with folded hands, paying homage to Christ and Almighty God, knowing that they will soon pass through the gate of death and bowing in silence to be with God.

During the worship, the significance of the suffering, crucifixion, death and resurrection of Jesus Christ became crystal clear in my mind and in my heart. Jesus' last words, "Father, into your hands I commit my spirit" (Luke 23:46), took on a special meaning at Nirmal Hriday for, ultimately, we all must surrender to God in death. Although suffering and death are the inheritance of mortality, Christ's resurrection was a glorious triumph giving purpose to pain and death and offering God's promise of eternal life. "For God so loved the world that he gave his one and only son, that whoever believes in him shall not perish but have everlasting life" (John 3:16). Verses from the Upanishads and Vedas, which a Hindu might pray when it is time to depart from this world, also flashed through my mind:

> Lead me from unreality to reality
> Lead me from darkness to light
> Lead me from death to immortality.[3]

> Now my breath and spirit goes to the Immortal,
>   and this body ends in ashes;
> OM. O Mind! Remember. Remember the deeds.
>   Remember the actions.[4]

The melodious voices of the sisters singing hymns in Bengali elevated the spirituality of this experience. Their song was a prayer of adoration and supplication for peace and tranquility, asking that all hearts and minds be open to God. "Here I am your servant" and "Thy will be done." As Jesus has said, even when two or three gather together in His name, He will be with them. The celebration of the Mass was a splendid silent meeting of the heart of oneness of spirit, affirming that something more beautiful awaits us after we pass through the door of death.

It was an inexplicable joy for me to have seen the expressions of peace and tranquility on the faces of the terminally ill destitutes at Nirmal Hriday. At Shishu Bhavan, I learned a lesson on life and, at Nirmal Hriday, a lesson on death. The question of mortality remains the same for every-one--are we ready to accept death at any time? Whether one faces death in Beverly Hills or in Nirmal Hriday, in comfortable surroundings or in poverty, each of us must face that crucial last experience of death alone with God. Mother Teresa has taught us that "the greatest aim of human life is to die in peace with God."

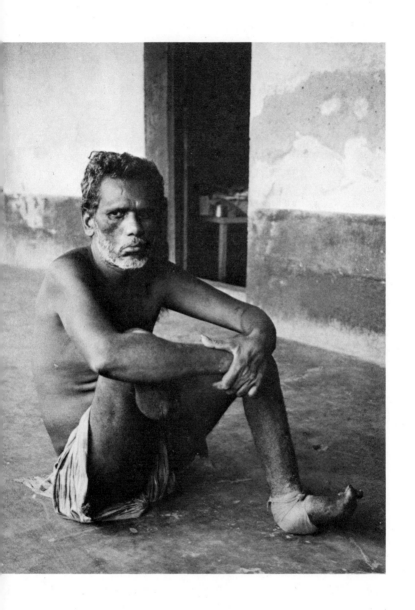

Address of

Mother Teresa of Calcutta

To the Graduating Class of Thomas Aquinas College

Santa Paula, California,

June 5, 1982

Transcript

Mother Teresa, M.C., speaks extemporaneously
without notes. This verbatim transcript was
prepared from a tape recording.

For ease in reading, Mother Teresa's address has
been paragraphed. In one or two instances, a word
has been inserted in brackets for clarity.

Commencement Address by Mother Teresa

In this beautiful day that our young people are looking forward to becoming carriers of God's love, let us ask Our Lady to give us her heart so beautiful, so pure, so immaculate; her heart so full of love and humility that we may be able to receive Jesus in the Bread of Life. Love Him as she loved Him and serve Him in the distressing disguise of the poor.

We read in the Scripture that God loved the world so much that He gave His Son as a proof of His love. And Jesus coming to Mary, the most beautiful of creatures, so pure, so holy. She, in accepting Him in her life, immediately, she went in haste to give Him to others.

And that haste today is very appropriate for you, for you, too, have received Jesus and have received of Jesus so many beautiful things from this college.

And now you go out: you also go in haste to give the joy of loving, the joy of sharing, for you have received not to keep but to share.

And what is there to share? What did Our Lady do? When she came into Elizabeth's house--that little unborn child--he was already six months in his mother's womb--that little, innocent, small, helpless child--was the first one to recognize the presence of Christ. And he leaped with joy. Even St. Joseph did not know that Mary had received Jesus. But this little one, so small, so innocent, so helpless. God used that little one to proclaim the greatness of His Son, the presence of His Son.

And this, the joy of the presence of Jesus, you must be able to give wherever you go. But you cannot give what you don't have. That's why you need a pure heart, a pure heart that you will receive as a fruit of your prayer, as a fruit of your oneness with Christ. And a pure heart can see God and if you see God immediately – immediately – you begin to love one another. That's all Jesus came on this earth to give us, that good news: "Love as I have loved you; love one another as I have loved you."

How wonderful it is to think that we all, all have been created for that purpose. We have not come into this world just to be a number. They say that we have many numbers in India. But we are not numbers. We are children of God. We have been created for a purpose, for greater things: to love and to be loved.

And therefore, that good news Jesus came to give us and that good news you must carry out, you must bring into the world where you are going to move in now. What good news? That God loves you and that you want to love others as He loves you, tenderly, lovingly.

And how do we know that God loves us? There is a very beautiful word in the Scripture in Isaias where He says: "I have called you by your name, you are Mine. Water will not drown you– fire will not burn you– I will give up nations for you. You are precious to Me. I love you. And even if mother could forget her child, I will not forget you. I have [carved] you in the palm of my hand." How wonderful it is, the tenderness of God's love for us. And it is this that you have to carry out in the world of today.

This expectation your parents, your relations, your friends, even the whole world, is expecting: that you be that light. The light that Jesus said: "I am the light that you must lit – I am the truth that you must speak – I am the joy that you must share – I am the life that you must lead – I am the love that you must love." Go with that: the joy of loving.

You must experience the joy of loving. And how do you experience that freedom? You need to be free to love; that means have a clean heart. And this is my prayer for you: that you become real carriers of God's love, in tenderness and love.

Do not be afraid. Do not be afraid to love. Even when suffering comes, humiliation comes, pain comes, success comes, joy comes. Remember, you are precious to Him. He loves you.

And this is something that today when we are brought together to proclaim: the joy of being loved and the joy of loving.

We hear so many terrible things happening. But never lose heart. We always – thank God, – I can smile. At least you can smile if nothing else.

I never forget one day I met a lady who was dying of cancer and I could see the way she was struggling with that terrible pain. And I said to her, I said, you know this is but the kiss of Jesus, a sign that you have come so close to Him on the cross that He can kiss you. And she joined her hands together and said. "Mother Teresa, please tell Jesus to stop kissing me."

This is the joy of suffering, the kiss of Jesus. Do not be afraid to share in that joy of suffering with Him because He will never give us more suffering than we are able to bear. I have seen that again and again with our poor people.

We deal with thousands of people, people who die of hunger, of disease, people who die of loneliness, of being unwanted, unloved. And I have never yet heard one of them complain or curse.

Once I picked up a man from the street, from an open drain, and I took him to our home and he did not shout, he did not blame anybody, just said: "I have lived like an animal in the street, but I am going to die like an angel, loved and cared [for]." Two or three hours after, he died with a big smile on his face — that was tenderness and love that came to him through the hands of those young sisters.

Now, in our congregation, we have about 70 young American sisters who have joined and who are completely so totally dedicated and through that taking care of the lepers, of the dying, of the crippled, of the unwanted, of the shutins and so on. And there is so much joy, that sharing and joy. Because Jesus wants us to be happy; He wants us to give that joy. "That My joy be with you." And He had more reason to be unhappy because we are loved by God himself even in suffering: it is not a punishment, it is a gift of God.

And so I think these days when you are — after so many years — four full years you are prepared — I hope you have learned to pray. And if you have learned to pray, that is your strength, that is your joy. And through this life of prayer make sure — the fruit of prayer is always the deepening of faith. And the fruit of faith is always love and the fruit of love is action. We must put our love for Jesus in the living action.

How do we do that? If we do it with Jesus, if we do it for Jesus, and if we do it to Jesus, then we know that we are with Him because He has said so.

This is not an act of faith, to believe that I am doing it to Jesus. Jesus has said, "Whatever you do to the least of my brethren, you do to Me."

And also the condition — in our last day when we come face to face with God, we are going to be judged by what we have been to Him. And He says: "I was hungry, you gave Me to eat; I was naked, and you clothed Me; I was homeless and you did it to Me." There is no imagination, no maybe.

Just as we believe that two and two make four — we don't need to believe that; we know it is like that. So [it is the] same when Jesus has said "You did it to Me," that presence. And to be able to do that, we need the Eucharist, we need Jesus in the Holy Communion, we need the Bread of Life. That's why Jesus made Himself [the] Bread of Life to satisfy our hunger for His love and then He makes Himself the Hungry One so that we can satisfy His hunger for our love.

A few months ago, I had to go to Delhi and one of the ministers was the top man in social works and he said: "Mother Teresa, you and we are doing [the] same social work. But there is a great difference between you and us. We do it for something and you do it to somebody."

You young people: remember, do it to somebody. That man, that woman; my brother, my sister: somebody. Jesus is distress in disguise.

And how do we do that?   Where does it begin, this love?   At home.   And how does this love begin?

[The] family that prays together, stays together.
And if you stay together, you will love one another
as God loves each one of you. As Jesus wants us to
love one another. Not in sadness, but in joy. To
think that I can love God in my brother, in my
sister. It is a wonderful thing.

Only we must come to know. Do we know the poor
of this beautiful country? Maybe the poor are in
our own family. Maybe we have somebody sick,
somebody old, somebody feeling very restless,
somebody feeling very lonely. Do we know that?

Here in the United States, our sisters are
working and it is surprising: there are not hungry
people, maybe, though we are feeding a big number
of people in New York--but, still, not so many in
Washington and other places. It is not that hunger
of Africa, of India, where people sometimes die of
hunger, but a terrible hunger for love, a terrible
loneliness, a terrible rejection that is a much
greater hunger.

Nakedness is not only for a piece of cloth, but
nakedness is a loss of that dignity, human dignity:
the loss for what is beautiful, what is pure, what
is chaste, what is virgin. Loss. Homelessness is
not only [for] a house made of bricks--homelessness
is being that people are completely forgotten,
rejected, left alone, as if they are nobody to
nobody.

I never forget, one day I was walking down the
streets of London and there I saw a man. The way
he was sitting, the way he was looking, he looked
the most rejected man that I have ever seen. So I
went right near him and I took his hand and shook
his hand. And my hands are always very warm except
here they are a little bit cold.

But I shook his hands and then he said: "Oh, after so long a time, I feel the warmth of a human hand." And his face was quite different. There was joy, there was sunshine in his eyes. I can't tell you the change that came on that man's life just with that simple shaking of the hand, the warmth of my hand. This is felt.

Now you young people must go out with that — with searching eyes: go in search and find. Maybe in your family; maybe next door neighbor. Find. There are many people here in the States.

To me, the greatest poverty is that abortion: the fear of the child. The child must die; the child must be killed so that we don't have to feed one more child, we don't have to educate one more child. Terrible! Terrible! Mother could murder her own child! Terrible! It is the sign of great poverty and so, open your eyes, come to know.

One evening, a man came to our house and said: "There is a family with eight children that have not eaten for a long time. Do something for them." And I took some rice and the mother took [it] — I could see from the eyes of the children — God knws how long they had not eaten — their eyes were simply shining with hunger, and big black lines under their eyes. And the mother went out with the rice and when she came back, I asked her: "Where did you go? And what did you do?" And she said: "They are hungry also." Next door neighbor. She knew they were hungry. I was not surprised that she gave but I was very much surprised that she knew because in a sorrow like that, in suffering like that, very often we have no time to think of others. And yet this tremendous woman had the courage to love like that, great love.

This is something that we have to learn from our poor people: they are very great people. You don't know what is hunger. You have never experienced that. But one day, I picked up a child, six, seven years old, from the street and I could see the pain of hunger in her face, so I gave her a piece of bread and then I saw the child eating the bread crumb by crumb. I said: "Eat, eat the bread." And then she looked at me and said, "I am afraid when the bread will be finished, I will be hungry again."

See, that little one, so small, has already tasted the pain of suffering, the pain of hunger. And this is what I want you, you who are going out into the world: open your eyes.

Many young people come to Calcutta to share in the work — many. From different universities, from different colleges, they come and spend two weeks, one month, according to what they are able to make. And there each one of them they come, share the life of prayer with us in our congregation and we have adoration every day, so for one in the evening.

So they come — especially want to work in the room for the dying and they come with us and they always say the same thing: "At home, I saw but I didn't look. You have taught me to see and to look. Now I go home and I am sure I will find the same, I will find people who need my tender love and care — all of them."

A girl — a university girl who was in her final examination — Ph.D. in Paris University. She came also. Before examination, she wanted to spend one month working with Mother Teresa in the room for the dying. She was always very occupied and so on. But then one week before, one day she came to our house and she put her hands around me and she said: "I found Jesus." I said, "Yes, where did you find Him?" And she said, "I found Him in the room for the dying." And I said to her, "What did you do with Jesus when you found Him?" And she said: "I went to confession and Holy Communion after 15 years." Then I said to her: "What else did you do with Jesus when you found Him?" And she said: "I sent a telegram to my parents and told them I found Jesus." So beautiful.

See: she came, she saw, she looked, and she did. This is what you go out with that determination – to give Jesus like Mary. When Mary came into the room with Elizabeth, the little one leaped with joy. Your presence should bring that in your own family first. The joy of that presence of Christ, the joy of purity, the joy of that real sharing.

It is very beautiful that a young man loves a young woman and a young woman loves a young man. That's a beautiful creation of God. But make sure that you love with a clean, with a pure heart, that you love with a virgin heart. And that on the day of your marriage when God makes you one – as in the Scripture we read that they cleave together and they become one – on that day that you can give to each other a virgin heart, a virgin body, a virgin soul – that is the greatest gift you can give to each other.

A few days before I left Calcutta, a young man and a woman came to our house and just two days before that they got married. And they gave me a big amount of money to feed the people because we cook for 7,000 people in Calcutta every day, so these good young people gave me the money to feed the people.

And I said to them: "Where did you get so much money?" And they said to me: "Mother, before our marriage, we decided that out of love for each other we will not buy wedding clothes, we will not have a wedding feast, we will give you the money." And I said, "Why, why did you do that?" Because that is unheard of in India, especially in a Hindu family. Marriage is a very important part of their lives. And they said they wanted to give something very special to each other: "We loved each other so tenderly and we wanted to give something special to each other." This is a love, a greater love.

So my prayer for you is that you go in the world today with a virgin heart, with a virgin love, and give that love to all you meet. Your presence should [light] a new light in the lives of the people.

When our sisters went to Yemen, in a Muslim country, completely Muslim, there is no church, no nothing there, and the governor of that place wrote and said: "The presence of the sisters has lit a new light in the lives of our people." This is something that you also —

Go forward with the joy and keep the joy of loving Jesus in your hearts and share that joy with all you meet especially with one another and with your family.

And through this love for each other you will grow in holiness. Holiness is not the luxury of the few. It's a simple duty for you and for me. So let us grow in that holiness so that one day we will be all one heart full of love in the Heart of Jesus.

And you also pray for us, the sisters and the brothers. We have consecrated our lives to love

Christ with undivided love and chastity through freedom of poverty in total surrender and obedience

And in our congregation we take a fourth vow of giving wholehearted free service to the poorest of the poor. By this vow, we are specially bound to the people who have nothing and nobody and also fully depend on Divine Providence.

We accept [no] government grants, no salaries, no church [supplements], we are just like the flowers of the field and the birds of the air. We depend on Him fully and He has been a wonderful Father to us and to our poor people.

We deal with thousands and thousands and thousands of people and we have never had to say "I'm sorry we don't have." It's always been there. So you pray that we don't spoil God's work, that it remains His work.

And you help your children when God calls them to join in giving their lives to God, to [the] priesthood or to religious life. Be grateful to God for this great gift, for this is something very special because God is asking your child to belong to Him totally and to give Him the all for Him.

So let us pray together for our poor people that God's love may be shown to them through each one of us.

Make us worthy, Lord, to serve our fellowmen throughout the world who live and die in poverty and hunger. Give them through our hands this day their daily bread and by the understanding love give peace and joy.

(© 1982, by Thomas Aquinas College. Published with the permission of Thomas Aquinas College.)

PART II: INDIA

A GLIMPSE OF HINDUISM

Hinduism has evolved as a natural expression of man's spiritual search through the ages. The basic tenets of Hinduism affirm the spirituality of man and propound that the realization of the inner Spirit is the highest aim in life. Hinduism is not a revealed religion, like Christianity or Islam, and it does not claim a personal redeemer. For a Hindu, there is one universal God and He has incarnated Himself in various forms throughout history. This belief in the multiple manifestations of the Supreme God has instilled the spirit of coexistence, tolerance and mutual respect for all religions in India. Hinduism is amorphous, many sided, and free from theological dogmas or rigorous commandments. It encompasses a vast array of beliefs, ranging from the veneration of idols to metaphysical speculations. Viewed from the aspect of intellectual understanding and reflection on God, man and the universe, Hinduism is a philosophy. When this knowledge and reflection are applied to daily life, Hinduism is a religion.

India has been a melting pot of different races, religions and ideologies for over five thousand years. Buddhism, Sikhism, Jainism, Islam, Christianity and Judaism have also become firmly entrenched in the Indian soil and these religions share a common cultural heritage with Hinduism. The spirit of Indian culture has been one of accommodation, giving concrete expression to the ideal of "live and let live." This chapter briefly describes some essential aspects of Hinduism.

The Three Paths To God

Jnana yoga is the path of knowledge which leads to the experience of the Supreme Godhead (Brahman). Brahman has been understood as the Supreme Spirit, the Universal Spirit and the Absolute, in contrast to Atman, which refers to the individual self or soul. Brahman is the all-pervading power in this universe and resides in each person as Atman. Therefore, man is primarily a spiritual being and the Sumum Bonum of life is to realize God within one's Self. Even though Brahman is manifest in every individual as Atman, it is not possible to realize Brahman in the experiences of day-to-day existence. The ordinary experiences are very limited in nature and distract us from the spiritual aspects of being. Empirical and scientific knowledge (Vignana) cannot lead us toward self-perfection and spiritual realization. The key which unlocks the door to the path of self-realization through knowledge is "integral knowledge," which transcends the limitations of the empirical and scientific realm.

In the Chandogya Upanishad, a beautiful passage explains the insufficiency of ordinary knowledge in comprehending the Absolute:

"Bring hither a fig from there."
"Here it is, sir."
"Divide it."
"It is divided, sir."
"What do you see there?"
"These rather (iva) fine seeds, sir."
"Of these, please (anga), divide one."
"It is divided, sir."
"What do you see there?"
"Nothing at all, sir."
Then he said to him: "Verily, my dear, that finest essence which you do not perceive . . . from

that finest essence this great Nyagrodha (sacred fig) tree thus arises . . .

That which is the finest essence--this whole world has that as its soul. That is Reality. That is Atman (Soul). That art thou, Svetaketu.[1]

In the day-to-day, mundane transactions, one identifies strongly with all kinds of activities. Just as an actor masks his true identity when he plays different roles, likewise, the self identifies with its activities. John may say that he is a businessman, a fundraiser for the Republican Party, a country western singer, and a volunteer worker with the mentally retarded. What John does defines his self-image. But John's various activities do not lead him to an understanding of the true identity of his self. The real self is hidden beneath the labyrinth of outer identifications. As long as the individual identifies his consciousness with the events and roles played in his life, he can lead a moral and just life but he will never discover his inner self in its unalloyed state.

The way of knowledge requires certain preliminary preparations in the quest for self-realization, namely, the rejection of selfishness and passion, the quieting of the emotions, purity of spirit, and striving to completely block off the mind and thoughts from the external world. "Know the soul to be the rider in the chariot which is the body. The intellect is the charioteer, and the mind the reins. The senses are the horses and the desirable things of the world are the thoroughfare on which they career. If the charioteer is unwise, and does not vigilantly restrain the mind, then the senses bolt uncontrollably like wicked horses. If, on the contrary, he is wise and keeps a firm hand on his mind, then the senses are in perfect control as a good horse with a competent charioteer."[2] And, furthermore, "higher than the senses are the objects of sense. Higher than the objects of sense is the mind (manas); and higher than the mind is the intellect (buddhi). Higher than the intellect is the Great Self (Atman)."[3]

The primary method employed in the path of knowledge is meditation (dhyana). In jnana yoga, concentration techniques are practiced which silence the faculties, one by one, thereby shutting off sense impressions, emotions and thinking. The Katha Upanishad teaches that "self-realization is the way to liberation. Turning the mind within and concentrating on the spirit, man should realize the divine character of his own soul and its intrinsic freedom. The Supreme Spirit is lodged within one's self, though unperceived because of the perplexities of joy and grief and attachment to worldly objects."[4]

When the meditator reaches a state of perfect concentration, he experiences the true nature of his self and the deeper reality of Supreme Consciousness occurs. The Upanishads describe this state as SAT, CHIT, and ANANDA (Being, Consciousness and Joy). Supreme consciousness, the highest state attainable through meditation, is the experience of the integration of Atman with Brahman. This peak spiritual experience is difficult to describe. "He is never seen, but is the Witness; He is never heard, but is the Hearer; He is never thought, but is the Thinker; He is never known, but is the Knower. There is no other witness but Him, no other hearer but Him, no other thinker but Him, no other knower but Him. He is the Internal Ruler, your own immortal self. Everything else but Him is mortal."[5] Atman and Brahman are two names for one truth. The truth of the universe is Brahman and our own inner truth is Atman.

In bhakti yoga, the cool contemplation of jnana yoga is replaced by hot devotion. The path of devotion is open to all, rich or poor, educated or illiterate, whereas only a few can follow the path of knowledge. The essence of devotion is prayer and prayer is the direct channel for communion with God. The individual does not seek identity with God but is a willing servant who seeks to experience His presence on a personal level. It is analogous to saying: "I want to taste sugar, but I don't want to be sugar." The way of bhakti has been beautifully described by Tukaram:

He who worships God must stand distinct from
Him
So only shall he know the joyful love of God.
For if he says that God and he are one
That joy, that love, shall vanish instantly
away.[6]

Bhakti is the most vital aspect of Hinduism and has kept Hinduism alive through the ages in spite of the fact that there are no established, organized dogmas or fixed modes of worship. The rich symbols, rituals, and hundreds of images of God are all outward expressions of the devotion in the hearts of the worshippers. The vast array of symbols and images of God, as well as the manifold modes of worship in India, quite often baffle Westerners. But, for a Hindu, every form of worship done in good faith is a true path to God and salvation. "In whatever form men worship Me, I look after them in that form. Men worship me in many ways, nevertheless, they all reach Me."[7] Hinduism teaches that God has manifested Himself in countless incarnations throughout history and He will continue to do so in the future. The devotee is free to choose any incarnation of God to worship, such as Brahma, Vishnu, Shiva, or any other form. The chosen deity becomes the devotee's "Ishta Devata."

The only prerequisite to following the path of devotion is faith (sraddha), the spirit of "letting go" with absolute trust in God. The devotee seeks the ecstasy of communion with God through prayer and worships God as the Lord and Master. What matters most is not to think theoretically about God but to love Him abundantly with one's whole being. It is the intensity of prayer and unconditional love for God that counts, not the duration of time spent in prayer.

God responds to the devotee with love, mercy and forgiveness and showers His grace (prasada) on man because it is His very nature to do so. However, man cannot demand God's mercy and grace. Both the virtuous and the sinners will be saved if they open up their hearts and seek the Lord. As Lord Krishna has said: "Even if a man of most sinful conduct loves Me with true and entire love, he must be regarded as a saint, for he has decided wisely. He will swiftly become completely righteous and obtain eternal peace. Know it for certain . . . that My loving devotee never perishes."[8]

In bhakti yoga, the devotee completely surrenders (prapatti) to God and finds final refuge (sharanagati) in Him. Faith, trust and refuge in God are not only a powerful antidote to existential anxiety, but also give comfort and peace in this life and salvation (moksha) in the next. "Set your heart on Me. Let your understanding enter into Me. You shall surely live with Me hereafter, of this there is no doubt."[9] Ultimately, God is the supreme judge in protecting the good and destroying the evil in this world. "For whenever there is a withering of righteousness and an uprising of unrighteousness on all sides, then I manifest Myself. For the deliverance of the righteous and the destruction of the evil doers and for the fulfillment of the moral law, I come into this world in every age.[10]

Hinduism is rich in bhakti literature and poetry, written in Sanskrit and many other Indian languages. Ramanand, Kabir, Nanak, Tulsidas, Namadev, Tukaram, Chaitanya, and the Alvars of the Tamilnad have composed splendid and heart-moving devotional songs of praise to God. The beautiful songs of these great devotees have inspired and brought solace to millions of Hindus in their daily spiritual quest.

The third avenue to God realization is through karma yoga, the path of action. In general, people live and work to economically prosper and to achieve personal goals and desires. In other words, actions are performed with strong motivations for success, recognition and achievement. Actions prompted by personal ends can often result in routineness, boredom, exhaustion, disappointment and failure. Attraction and repulsion, likes and dislikes, are all natural outcomes associated with actions carried out from the pragmatic point of view. According to the Bhagavad Gita, there is nothing wrong with working only for rewards and personal satisfaction but such actions are, at most, only second best. The goal of karma yoga, the highest form of action, is to perform all work gladly for God without personal motivations. One need not be a recluse to attain God realization but can find Him in the busy daily world of actions.

When actions are offered as an active service to the Lord, work ceases to be a burden and it becomes a sacred, loving sacrifice. The individual no longer ponders over the possible final results of action but, rather, gives himself freely and totally in the process of action itself. The scheme of life built on selfish hopes and desires is transformed into a higher plane and the Divine Will guides all actions. Thus, action is transformed into dynamic action, which is the bedrock of

life and brings out the full potential latent in
man, leading to physical, psychological, and
spiritual fulfillment. Joy, creativity and peace
are the natural results of dynamic action because
the mind is freed from all calculations and pre-
occupations with thinking. Countless great men and
women have served humanity throughout history by
selflessly carrying out actions as a dedication to
God. Selfish actions perish with the individual,
whereas selfless actions leave inspirational foot-
prints for posterity.

The main message of karma yoga is that one
should develop renunciation in action but not
renunciation of action. This specifically means
that one who works for God is detatched from any
results of his actions. "You have a right only to
work, never to its fruits; let not the fruit of
your work be your motive; nor let there be in you
any attachment to inactivity."[11] Renunciation in
action is possible only after one transcends selfishness and looks at good and bad fortune, gain and
loss, victory and defeat, with equanimity and
accepts all as the will of God. "Always do your
work with detachment. By such performance of
duties without attachment man attains bliss."[12]
Those who follow the way of action are freed from
attraction and repulsion and the anxieties and
sorrows of life. They experience the peace and joy
of offering their lives and their energies to God.

Whatever you do, whatever you enjoy,
whatever you sacrifice, whatever you give
away, whatever penance you practice, . . .
do it . . . as an offering to Me.
Thus shall you be liberated from the
bonds of actions, which bear good and evil
results. With your mind firmly set in the
way of renunciation, you will become free
and reach Me.[13]

The way of action teaches that we can overcome any turmoil and challenge in life by fulfilling our moral obligations and leaving the rest to God. When actions are elevated to the level of consecration to God, all actions become holy and work itself becomes a form of devotion. As Mother Teresa says, "You must find your holiness in what you are doing . . . find your holiness in your work."[14]

The Four Values of Man

Many Westerners hold the mistaken notion that Hinduism is ascetic, other-worldly, fatalistic, and looks down upon the pleasures of life. Some people even believe that India is full of yogis and meditators and that Hindus have no desire to live a comfortable life or to work hard for material prosperity. These mistaken ideas have led some to conclude that poverty is the result of the preoccupation with Hindu asceticism and spirituality! Nothing could be further from the truth. Most modern Indian philosophers, who have popularized Hinduism and Indian philosophy, have interpreted the traditional texts strictly from the Advaitic, or idealistic, point of view. Generally, they have not interpreted Hinduism and Indian philosophy as a catalytic force which could revive realistic and pragmatic ethical values for the advancement of the country.

Hinduism is not a religion of theological dogma but a way of life which affirms the meaning of existence in this world and beyond. It endorses a balanced view of life and the fulfillment of man's material, psychological, spiritual and physical needs. The four values of man (Purusharthas) are dharma, artha, kama, and moksha. The Purusharthas have been set forth as pragmatic moral guidelines which both affirm the enjoyment and fulfillment of human potentialities and point out the individual's responsibilities and obligations toward self, the family and society.

Dharma, which means justice, law, duty, virtue and social obligation, is a complex ethical concept which lends itself to various interpretations. Dharma has originated from the Sanskrit word "dhr" which connotes "to bear," "to carry," "that which supports," or "that which upholds." Dharma is the expression of the Vedic conception of cosmic moral order (rta). It is both eternal and immutable, having been set in place by the Creator, and it is the most important value in Hinduism. Dharma "refers not only to the whole context of law and custom (religion, usage, ethics, good works, virtue, religious or moral merit, justice, piety, impartiality), but also to the essential nature, character or quality of the individual, as a result of which his duty, social function, vocation or moral standard is what it is."[15]

Dharma is the cause of the maintenance of the universe, as well. "Dharma was declared for the sake of non-violence towards beings; therefore that which is conducive to the non-violence towards beings is certainly dharma. Dharma is (so)-called because it upholds all creatures . . . Therefore that which is capable of upholding is dharma."[16] And, "dharma was declared for the sake of advance-ment of beings (bhuta)."[17]

Dharma is primarily discussed in the context of moral precepts. The practice of non-violence (ahimsa), the pursuit of truth (satya), the control of the senses (indriyanigraha), charity (dana), tolerance (kshanti), self-control (dama), and compassion (daya) are means of realizing dharma in daily life. As the primary regulator of life, dharma exemplifies the ideal social order, wherein each person contributes and plays a constructive role in relation to the others in the society. In essence, all actions come within the periphery of dharma, hence, dharma must be vigilantly pursued. The Bhagavid Gita points out that each person has an obligation to carry on his or her dharma solely for the sake of duty. When one acts according to dharma, the rewards or results are immaterial. Individual duty (svadharma) refers to one's contribution of predominantly positive qualities for the good of society as a whole. Caring for one's suffering fellowmen is also dharma. Man has an obligation to do his duty for the sake of the good of the whole society (loka samgraha) because disorder and discord of any kind in this world is a threat to existence.

Dharma gives strength and power to carry on work without anguish or hesitancy because actions carried out for the sake of duty and morality free the individual from worry about the results. Yudhisthira says in the Mahabharata: "I never act, solicitous of the fruits of my actions, I give away, because it is my duty to give, I sacrifice, because it is my duty to sacrifice. I accomplish to the best of my power whatever a person living in domesticity should do, regardless of the fact whether those acts have fruits or not . . . The man who wishes to reap the fruits of virtue is a trader of virtue."[18]

The primary ethical principle of dharma is eternal and never changes, whereas the contents of dharma are subject to change. The contents of dharma are the practical moral issues which evolve with the changes in societies and cultures. The contents of dharma must not remain static. Otherwise, both the ethical and pragmatic purpose of dharma is lost. For example, the varna system, which was prescribed for the smooth functioning of society in ancient India, had positive ethical value and purpose. But, by the time varna dharma deteriorated into the hereditary caste system, its moral import and merit had completely disappeared.

The main aspects of dharma can be summarized in two concepts. Firstly, dharma is that through which the welfare (abhyudaya) of the society is attained and, secondly, dharma is that through which the highest good (nishreya) hereafter is attained. Dharma is closely connected with the doctrine of karma, as explained in the Brihadaranyaka Upanishad. The law of karma states that we will become what we do. The person who does good actions becomes virtuous and, likewise, the person who performs bad actions becomes evil.[19] Karma is the cosmic law of cause and effect, whereby we reap what we sow. According to Hindu belief, the moral repercussions of present actions will bear fruit in the next reincarnation. Likewise, one's status in this life is the result of actions done in the previous life. The doctrine of samsara, or reincarnation, plays a powerful role in encouraging morality and good behavior, for righteousness is the only way to escape future suffering and bad karma. As Shankaracharya persuasively puts it, "unless a person is aware of the existence of the self in a future life, he will not be inclined to attain what is good in this life and avoid what is evil."[20]

The second purushartha is artha, which is generally defined as material possessions and wealth. Artha literally means money (rai), or thing (vastu). Rangaswami Aiyangar defines it as "any material object capable of satisfying a human desire . . . The Indian conceptions of artha and dhanam, with their variants, correspond closely to the most modern conceptions of 'goods' and 'wealth.'"[21] The Artha Shastra (treatise on economics) is a magnificent ancient work dealing with worldly success and the acquisition of wealth, intended for both individuals and rulers.

In the Smrti tradition, artha is the most important value for the maintenance and success of the individual.   Moksha (salvation) is a far-fetched ideal for a man who has no means of livelihood and artha is considered a primary prerequisite to the realization of dharma and kama (pleasure). However, riches should be pursued as a means to an end, not as an end in itself, for artha is sub-servient to dharma.   Shankaracharya says: "The wise one should acquire arthas in such a way that they do not conflict with dharma, then only is this wealth good (ucita) for giving to others and enjoying oneself; otherwise it is the abuse of artha."[22]

Even the original tenents of Buddhism, although set forth for a monastic order, comment on the importance of artha.   "Wealth being obtained by one's hard work, accumulated by the strength of one's hands, earned by one's sweat, righteously obtained (thinking, 'I have this wealth'), one becomes happy."[23]

The Panchatantra, a volume of Indian folk tales, poetically praises money and its value:

A fangless snake; an elephant
without an ichor-store;
A man who lacks a cash account--
are names and nothing more[24]

The wealthy, though of meanest birth,
Are much respected on the earth;
The poor whose lineage is prized
Like clearest moonlight, are despised.[25]

Pleasure and happiness, in general, are what every human being wants in life. Kama refers to both sexual enjoyment and other sensual and asthetic pleasures. Hinduism considers kama as an important value in life because one's natural desires for sexual pleasure must be satisfied to lead a normal life. Denial of desire and sexuality does not eliminate it but, instead, suppresses the desire and leads to unhealthy dissatisfaction. Consequently, frustration and dissatisfaction hinder the development of the full human potential within the individual.

During Hindu marriage ceremonies, the bridegroom takes an oath: "I shall not neglect her in dharma, artha and kama" (dharme ca arthe ca kame ca naticarmani). The population explosion is clear evidence that Indians are living up to the realization of kama!

The Kama Sutra of Vatsayana, written around the fourth century A.D., is a remarkable treatise which gives detailed descriptions of the many ways to enjoy sexual love. The Kama Sutra's definition of pleasure is "the enjoyment of appropriate objects by the five senses of hearing (srotra), feeling (tvak), seeing (caksu), tasting (jihva), and smelling (ghrana), assisted by the mind (manas) together with the soul (atman)."[26]

Although sexual pleasures enjoyed by married couples are not condemned by Hinduism, pleasure has not been endorsed as the highest aim in life, for enjoyment is only transitory. Too much attachment to the pursuit of enjoyment results in pain and unhappiness. To quote the Mahabharata, "desires are never satisfied by indulging in them but they flare up like fire in which butter is poured."[27] Again, in the Artha Shastra, Kautilya says that "one may enjoy kama provided that there is no conflict (virodha) with dharma and artha. One should not deprive oneself of pleasures."[28] In summary, artha and kama are necessary ingredients to life but they should be subservient to dharma and moksha.

Mahatma Ghandi took quite the opposite stand on the value of sex and wealth. "Money renders a man helpless. The other thing which is equally harmful is a sexual vice. Both are poison. A snake bite is a lesser poison than these two because the former merely destroys the body but the latter destroys the body, mind, and soul."[29] In Hinduism, celibacy has traditionally been practiced by individuals who want to join a monastic order or who wish to intensively pursue spirituality. But Ghandi attempted to turn India into a land of puritans by insisting upon abstinence from sex even by married people. Why should a couple marry in the first place if they want to remain celibate? The limitations and impracticality of Ghandi's interpretation of Hinduism are readily apparent.

Some Hindu sages have pointed out that the absence of pain and suffering is the state of happiness and they have warned about the potential dangers of sensuality. "Let one who desires happiness (sukha) be controlled (samyata) and take refuge in perfect contentment (santosa); contentment is truly the root of happiness. The opposite is the root of sorrow (duhkha).[30]

Moksha, the ultimate goal of Hinduism, means freedom, salvation, realization, self-perfection, and fulfillment. Paul Deussen aptly remarks that moksha is "the most precious jewel of Indian faith." Artha, kama and dharma reach fruition and fulfillment in moksha, which is called parama-purushartha (the highest wealth).

A distinction is made between liberation while alive (jivan mukti) and liberation after death (videha mukti). Jivan mukti means that one need not wait for the end of life to attain salvation. The Brihadaranyaka Upanishad states that "when all desires (kama) entirely disappear, a mortal (mrtya) becomes immortal (amrta) and realizes the Brahman even here (atra)."[31] Shankara comments that liberation while alive is a state wherein the phenomenal world ceases to exist, although it is as before, and the liberated person is influenced neither by pain or by pleasure.

The quest for salvation is the quintessence of Hinduism and the three ways to God--jnana, bhakti, and karma yoga--are the means of attaining it. Moksha is man's ultimate destiny, giving final release from the cycle of births and deaths, struggle and suffering.

SOCIAL PROBLEMS OF INDIA

Caste and Untouchability

The origin of the caste system can be traced to the ancient Hindu hymns of the Vedas, which were composed around 4500 B.C.

According to the Vedic theory of creation, the Supreme Being manifested himself in this universe by dividing his body into four parts, thus creating four types of men, the Brahmins (the priestly class), the Kshatriya (the warrior or ruling class), the Vaisyas (the business class), and the Shudras (the agriculture and labor class).

His mouth became the Brahmin
His arms the Kshatriya
His thighs became Vaisya
And Shudra was born from his feet.[1]

This fourfold division of creation is known as the varna system. In the broad sense of the term "varna" means social stratification. Since each group was created by God, each and every member of the four groups has divinity in him. Ideally, the Vedic theory of creation categorized the four groups of qualities and human potentialities that were necessary for the functioning of the society. During the early Vedic period, moral character and talent determined the class to which each person belonged and intermarriage and flexibility of customs were common.

Each social group was required to carry on particular duties as a moral obligation, thereby contributing to social harmony and order. The Vedic moral imperatives for each of the four classes are known as varna dharma and the following is a brief description of each group's traditional obligations:

1. Brahmin — The priestly class was obliged to study and teach the Vedas and to perform sacrificial religious rituals. Their primary duties were to teach and disseminate knowledge and to pursue spirituality.

2. Kshatriya — The class of rulers and warriors were charged with protecting the righteous, even if they must go to war. Kshatriyas were allowed to perform religious sacrifices and to study the Vedas under the guidance of a Brahmin priest. However, they were not allowed to officiate at religious ceremonies as a priest or to teach the sacred scriptures. Primarily, members of this class were obliged to pursue valorous deeds and set examples of strength and prowress.

3. Vaishya — The class of businessmen were obliged to carry on trade and to give gifts to the Brahmins and Kshatriyas. This class was also allowed to perform certain religious sacrifices and to study the Vedas under the guidance of a Brahmin priest.

4. Shudra — The class of agriculturists were subordinate to the other three classes and their main duty was to

serve the upper classes. Shudras were
forbidden to participate in any
religious sacrifices or ceremonies.

The Brahmins, Kshatriyas, and Vaishyas are
called dwijas (twice-born) because they are privi-
leged to undergo a religious rebirth at puberty,
known as the ceremony of the initiation of the
sacred thread (upanayana). The sacred thread
ceremony inaugurates a young man into the study of
the Scriptures. Each family in the dwijas groups
has a Gotra which traces their spiritual lineage to
an ancient seer or priest.

When the Vedic religion became established as a
ritualistic system, the classes of priesthood and
aristocracy were separated from the common people.
The twice-born were obligated to strive toward
perfection and self-purification by carrying out
their social and religious duties. Anyone who did
not belong to the three upper castes were barred
from participation in the religious rituals and
sacrifices of the Hindu community. The Brahmins
wrote the Vedas to promote their own interests and
cleverly freed themselves from the toils of existence. Some even claimed divine status:

Verily there are two kind of Gods
For the Gods themselves are assuredly Gods
And the priests who have studied and teach
Vedic lore are the human Gods.[2]

The Manu Dharma Shastra (Hindu Law), completed
around 300 A.D., has been considered by Brahmin
scholars to be the most important text in Hinduism
apart from the Vedas. Manu, its author, strengthened the Vedic concept of social stratification and
the status of the Brahmins. "The Gods are invisible deities, but Brahmins are visible
deities."[3] Manu set forth the code of conduct for

each class and gave elaborate details of punishment for those who broke the laws pertaining to their social class. Naturally, the Brahmins were given lenient punishment for their offenses when compared with the punishment prescribed for the other three groups.

The theory of karma, which states that one's current birthright and fortune is the result of good or bad deeds in a previous life, strengthened and promoted the idea of hereditary caste. The concepts of rebirth, transmigration and fatalism had tremendous impact upon the people and each silently accepted their caste status because they firmly believed that it was of their own making. The karma theory intimidated the lower castes into following their prescribed duties. Otherwise, they feared being reborn into an even lower strata in the next life. The higher castes used the theory of karma to reinforce their claims of superiority. Birth into a higher caste implied that one was destined to enjoy life and to be served because of his good deeds in a former incarnation.

If the Vedic theory of creation had been given to man through divine revelation, the concepts contained in the theory should have been unique. But, the Greek philosopher, Plato, presented the same ideas in the Republic, which further shows that the varna system was a human creation, rather than being of divine origin. Plato wrote that the ideal state consisted of a hierarchy with the Guardian (the philosopher-king) at the top, the Auxiliaries (the military) in the middle, and the Artisans at the bottom of the hierarchy. Plato's three classifications correspond to the Brahmin, the Kshatriya, and the Vaishya classes. Plato also endorsed the institution of slavery in his Laws. The only difference between the two theories is that Plato failed miserably in establishing his ideal state, whereas the Varna System was accepted in India and became a rigid social institution.

Eventually, the varna system of social categories solidified into a rigid caste system. Caste became hereditary and a permanent part of Hindu society. After the caste system became firmly entrenched, innumerable subdivisions, known as jati, formed within each caste. Just as the castes are vertically categorized by status, so too are the subdivisions (jati) arranged in a vertical hierarchy. In India today, each caste has numerous subdivisions and over 3,000 jati exist among the four castes.

Tragically, not all members of Hindu society were included in the hereditary scheme of the four castes. Those who were left out were classified as Untouchables. This group is the most neglected and discriminated against in Hindu society. For centuries, the higher castes have treated the Untouchables worse than animals. Even today, these poor people are forced to live outside the community and are isolated socially and culturally. Only "polluted," menial jobs were assigned to the Untouchables, such as discarding feces (before the advent of modern plumbing), curing hides, carting garbage and street scavenging. Some cultivated arid land to earn a meager livlihood but only a microscopic minority of Untouchables were given this opportunity. Restrictions and prohibitions, which varied from province to province, controlled the movements, mode of life and rules of servitude of the Untouchables. They were forbidden to enter the temples, to use water from the public wells, and even to walk down the streets where the upper castes resided.

The history of the Untouchables in India is sad and shameful. The caste system completely lacks

any justice or legal recourse for the Shudras and
the Untouchables and the treatment given them over
the centuries has been inhuman and ungodly to the
core. There is clear evidence that the caste
system was deep-rooted in India even as early as
500 B.C. One of the followers of Gautama Buddha,
Sunita by name, was an outcaste. The fact that the
status of outcaste was in existence during Buddha's
lifetime indicates that casteism and untouchability
have been prevalent in Indian society for many
generations.

Mahatma Gandhi, the father of India's independence movement and the champion of non-violence,
was the first Hindu to politically strive to uplift
the Untouchables. He coined a new name for the
Untouchables, Harijans, which means "children of
God." At no time in India's history were the
people so united as under Gandhi's leadership.
However, he did a great disservice to the country
by not calling for the abolition of the caste
system in order to integrate Hindu society. Gandhi
could have brought about powerful positive social
changes and created the opportunity for social
mobility. Instead, as a Hindu puritan and funda-
mentalist, he wholeheartedly endorsed the caste
system. Mahatma Gandhi affirmed every basic tenent
of Hinduism. To quote his words: "I call myself a
Sanatani Hindu, because (a) I believe in the Vedas,
the Upanishads, the Puranas and all that goes by
the name of Hindu scriptures and therefore in
Avatars (incarnations) and rebirth; and (b) I
believe in the Varna Dharma."[4]

Gandhi visualized the integration of the Untouchables with the fourth caste, the Shudras.
"Caste I consider a useful institution if properly
regulated. Untouchability is a crime against God
and humanity. I would purify the former, I would

destroy the latter."[5]   Gandhi extolled the significance of the caste system as the "truest road to
equality, it [Hinduism] is a religion not of self-
indulgence but of self-sacrifice.   It is a religion
not of insolence but of humility."[6]   He supported
the hereditary status of caste, as well, for "Varna
Dharma (caste morality) implies that every one must
remain content with his hereditary means of livelihood."[7]

Mahatma Gandhi's struggle to merge the Untouchable groups with the Shudra caste was a massive
failure.   However, his contributions were positive
in that it was the first time any higher caste
Hindu had publicly tried to improve the lot of the
Untouchables.

A contemporary of Gandhi, Bhimrao Ramji
Ambedkar, succeeded by legal means in uplifting the
status of the Untouchables in Indian society.
Ambedkar belonged to the Mahers, which is a large
Untouchable community in Maharastra State.   He was
a bright student and was fortunate to have been
awarded a grant from the Gaikwad of Baroda to
pursue his studies at Princeton University.   The
Gaikwad of Baroda, a wealthy Hindu philanthropist,
provided financial assistance for the education of
promising Untouchable youths.   While at Princeton
University, Ambedkar earned M.A. and Ph.D. degrees.
He then obtained a D.Sc. from London University and
entrance to the Bar from Grey Inn of London.   In
1923, Dr. Ambedkar returned to his homeland and
began working for the cause of the Untouchables.
His fight for legal and political rights for his
countrymen was a long, bitter struggle.

The Gandhian ideal of incorporating the Un-
touchables into the Shudra caste was repugnant to
Ambedkar.   He was understandably infuriated that
Gandhi, who was born into the Bania upper caste and

who had never experienced society's rejection, should preach that all Untouchables belong in the group of farmers and general laborers. According to Gandhi, "one born a scavenger must earn his livelihood by being a scavenger, and then do whatever else he likes. For a scavenger is as worthy of his hire as a lawyer or your president. That according to me is Hinduism."[8]

Dr. Ambedkar told Gandhi on August 13, 1931, "Gandiji, I have no homeland . . . How can I call this land my homeland and this religion my own wherein we are treated worse than cats and dogs, wherein we cannot get water to drink? No self-respecting Untouchable worth the name will be proud of this land."[9] In another speech, Ambedkar charged that "to the Untouchables, Hinduism is a veritable chamber of horrors." Dr. Ambedkar publicly protested the segregation of the Untouchables and established the Peoples' Education Society to promote their cause. He even burned the ancient Hindu law book, Manusmriti, in 1927, as a protest against casteism.

During the British occupation of India, Dr. Ambedkar fought for the allottment of separate electorates for the depressed classes (Untouchables) and special representation through reserved seats in the parliament. Mahatma Gandhi threatened to "fast unto death" if the British provided special privileges for the Untouchables when they granted independence to India.

In 1942, Dr. Ambedkar established a new political party, The Scheduled Castes Federation, for the Untouchables, and, in 1947, when India gained independence, Dr. Ambedkar became law minister and wrote the constitution of India. What an irony of history that an Untouchable wrote the law of the land! In utter dismay and disgust

towards the inhuman Hindu institution of caste, Dr.
Ambedkar embraced Buddhism in 1956 and was joined
in his new religion by three million followers.

After India attained independence in 1947, the
federal government implemented concrete and constructive programs to erase the social stigma of
untouchability and to give the Untouchables an
opportunity to economically advance. Laws were
passed which forbade discrimination in all areas of
society and criteria for preferential job reserva-
tions and entrance to educational institutions were
established for the downtrodden and the outcastes.

The Indian government officially labeled the
untouchable groups as "scheduled castes." This
category encompasses the exterior castes, the
untouchable groups, the depressed classes, and the
outcastes (harijans). The neglected and primitive
tribal peoples who were located in the jungles and
remote areas of India have also been included in
the programs for social upliftment. In addition,
some State governments have made provisions for
other backward classes, thereby including those who
rank below the lowest caste Hindus and above the
Untouchables. Legal protections have been incorporated into the Indian constitution to aid the
depressed classes. The following is a brief description of the major laws:

1. the abolition of 'untouchability' and the
   forbidding of its practice in any form (art.
   17);
2. permitting the State to make reservation for
   the backward classes in public services in
   case of inadequate representation and re-
   quiring the State to consider the claims of
   the scheduled castes and tribes in the
   making of appointments to public services
   (art. 16 and 335);

3. prohibition of traffic in human beings and forced labour (art. 23);

4. the removal of any disability, liability, restriction or condition with regard to access to shops, public restaurants, hotels and places of public entertainment or the use of wells, tanks, bathing ghats, roads and places of public resort maintained wholly or partly out of State funds or dedicated to the use of the general public (art. 15);

5. the throwing open by law of Hindu religious institutions of a public character to all classes and sections of Hindus (art. 25);

6. special representation in the Lok Sabha and the state Vidhan Sabhas to scheduled castes and tribes until 25 January 1990 (arts. 164 and 338 and Fifth Schedule);

7. the promotion of their educational and economic interests and their protection from social injustice and all forms of exploitation (art. 46);

8. . . . any denial of admission to educational institutions maintained by the State or receiving aid out of State funds (art.29);[10]

The preferential advantages and privileges for the Untouchable groups are offered only to those who are Hindus. The stance taken by the Indian government is that when an Untouchable converts to Christianity or Islam, he is no longer an Untouchable and he ceases to be a member of the Scheduled Castes and Tribes. The unfortunate irony of the situation is that the caste system is entrenched even among the Christians and the Muslims.

Indian Muslims recognize two main social divisions, the high and the low Muslims.[11] In the state of Bengal, for example, there are Ashraf and Ajlab Muslims. Ashraf means "noble" and refers to the descendants of Muslims of foreign origin and converts from the high Hindu castes. Ajlab means "wretches" and encompasses all Muslim converts from the lower castes and the Untouchables.

In the state of Kerala, where Christianity has strong roots, the distinction between high and low Christians is an accepted reality. The word, "putuchristiani," which literally translates as "new converts," is used to specifically refer to Hindu converts to Christianity from the lower castes and the Untouchables. Even though many lower caste and Untouchable families became Christians five generations ago, their descendants are still considered as putuchristiani to distinguish them from the Syrian Christians who have been converted from the higher Hindu castes. Recent Hindu converts to Christianity from the upper castes are never referred to as putuchristiani but always as Syrian Christians. There are a large number of Christians in the southern districts of Madras who even claim that they are truer adherents to the caste system than the Hindus themselves! Marriages within the Christian community take place on the basis of caste lineage. Even though the practice of caste discrimination is unchristian and churches in India do not endorse such practices, the customs continue.

The Untouchable groups of Christians face a double handicap. Firstly, they are discriminated against by their fellow Christians and, secondly, they cannot qualify for the privileges offered to Hindu Untouchables. As a result, many have re-converted to Hinduism, much to the dismay of the Christian churches.

Today, the Scheduled Castes and Tribes face three major problems—the stigma of untouchability, poverty, and lack of power in the society.

Approximately 23 percent (175 million) of the Indian population belong to the Scheduled Castes and Tribes and, if the Backward Classes are counted, these two groups make up about 40 percent of the total population.[12] The Indian government has made considerable progress over the past three decades and continues its commitment toward improving their economic and social status. For example, 6 billion rupees have been allotted to Scheduled Castes' special assistance for the years 1980-1985. Millions of rupees have been funded for education, agriculture, and housing assistance. Visible progress has been eclipsed, however, by the population explosion among the poor, and the need to uplift them remains a major goal of the government. Also, a number of voluntary organizations, such as Harijan Sewak Sangh, the Bharatiya Depressed Class League in New Delhi, the Ramakrishna Mission in West Bengal, the Servants of India Society in Poona, Andhra Rashtra Adima Jati Sevak Sangh in Nellore, and others are working to improve the conditions of life for the Scheduled Castes and Tribes.

The politics of Untouchability has taken a peculiar twist. Certain groups are clamoring to be classified as members of the Scheduled Castes and Tribes. Innumerable subcastes, who technically can be considered as caste Hindus, are eagerly pursuing the status of backwardness in order to receive government scholarships, subsidies, jobs and reserved representation in the legislature. Prime Minister Gandhi, when addressing the All-India Conference of state ministers in charge of the Backward Classes' welfare, commented: "We should be against making backwardness a vested interest. We thought the word 'backwardness' would gradually go out of our vocabulary but we find more and more people seeking to get listed as backward. This is a backward looking approach."[13]

The practice of choosing an occupation based upon hereditary caste, i.e., the priesthood, the military, business or agriculture, is rapidly disappearing as a result of the advent of science and technology, modernization and industrialization. Brahmins have entered into occupations which were once performed by the lower castes and members of the other castes now hold high positions in the government, the universities, and private business enterprise. In fact, the Brahmin priesthood is rapidly dwindling because the renumeration for religious services is low and the traditional Hindu rituals are no longer in great demand, with the exception of marriages and death ceremonies. In essence, hereditary profession based upon caste has become obsolete.

However, casteism is deeply entrenched in the political sphere in the struggle for political and economic power. Caste affiliation has become the main channel of communication among its members and is the primary springboard for political leadership. Voting along caste lines has reinforced caste consciousness and loyalties. Caste communalism and caste nepotism have become rampant in Indian society. When Dr. S. Radhakrishnan was the President of India, he wrote:

> Caste has ceased to be a social evil but has become a political and administrative evil. We want to get votes and we set up candidates suited to the people who have a vote. If it is a Nadar constituency we set up a Nadar; if it is a Harijan constituency we set up a Harijan. If it is a Kamma constituency we set up a Kamma. This is what we have been doing. It is therefore essential that politics should be as far as possible lifted out of this kind of morass.[14]

The same idea was reiterated by S. Chandrashekar, a former minister in Prime Minister Indira Gandhi's cabinet: "While India is the world's largest democracy, the influence of caste on the choice of the candidates to contest elections is negating the democratic ideal. The political parties without exception set up candidates belonging to the caste of the majority of the constituency concerned."[15]

There are no easy, simple solutions to the social problems of casteism and untouchability. Today, Indian society needs the unifying force of the revival of moral values, integrity, and respect for the individual, with dedicated commitment to work for the good of all. Only then will casteism die a natural death.

Overpopulation

Overpopulation in India is a burning problem which perplexes the government, the economists, and the demographers. India's national destiny is closely interwoven with the silent population explosion. Providing adequate food, housing, education, and employment for the expanding population is becoming an insurmountable task and is the major obstacle to the economic and social development of India. China has already crossed the mark of one billion people and India is next in line:

        China - over 1 billion population
        India - 684 million population
        U.S.S.R. - 267 million population
        U.S.A. - 226 million population

When India attained independence in 1947, the population was 340 million. According to the 1981 census, it has now burgeoned to 684 million, i.e., within the short span of 34 years, the population has doubled (refer Table I). In just one decade,

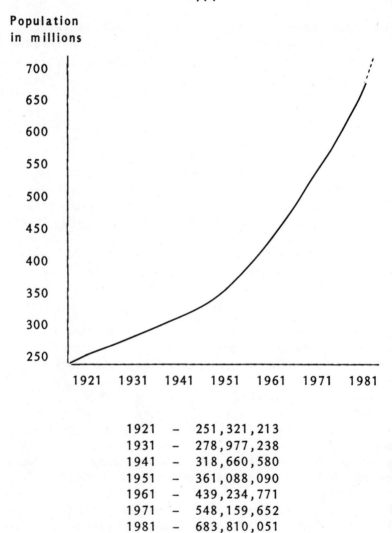

1921	–	251,321,213
1931	–	278,977,238
1941	–	318,660,580
1951	–	361,088,090
1961	–	439,234,771
1971	–	548,159,652
1981	–	683,810,051

TABLE I

India's Population Growth 1921 – 1981

between 1971 and 1981, the Indian population has increased by 134 million, an increase which equals the total population of Canada and one-half the total population of the United States! Each month, 1.11 million babies are born in India and at this rate, there will be over one billion Indians before the year 2000.

The problem of overpopulation is not unique to India alone. Rapid population growth is reaching crisis proportions in most underdeveloped countries in Asia, Africa and Latin America, for these countries are burdened with an average population growth of 3.5 percent or more per year. Statistics show that when the population increases at 1 percent per year, it will double in size within 70 years; 2 percent growth will double the population in 35 years; and 3.5 percent growth will double it in less than 20 years. From 1951 to 1981, India had an average annual population growth rate of over 2 percent. In the past 30 years, the birth rate in India has annually exceeded the death rate, due in part to better health care and the availability of adequate nurishment.

Guided by the twin objectives of self-reliance and sustained economic growth, the Indian government has successfully piloted Five Year Plans since 1951.[16] The Five Year Plans operate within the framework of the Directive Principles of State Policy as set forth in the Indian Constitution. The government's Five Year Plans complement private free enterprise in developing programs to improve agriculture, industry and social welfare. These programs have raised the average standard of living considerably and have effectively utilized available natural resources and human potential to reduce inequalities in income and to fight the problems of poverty and unemployment. As a result, India has achieved self-sufficiency in food

production, as well as advancement in science,
technology and industrialization. The exportation
of Indian goods has dramatically increased, free
health facilities have been opened throughout the
country, and there has been a marked increase in
literacy and longevity. In fact, the overall
literacy rate now stands at 36 percent of the
population, a substantial improvement over the 17
percent literacy rate in 1951. Additionally, India
is emerging as a major political force in Asia and
is offering economic and technological aid to other
Asian and African countries. But these achievements cannot possibly overtake the population
explosion and poverty has increased proportionally
with the growth of the population.

Although poverty is visible throughout India,
the intense desolation and hopelessness of Calcutta
cannot be found elsewhere in the country. Some of
the reasons for Calcutta's unique situation have
been previously discussed. The total population of
Calcutta was estimated to be nine million in 1981,
of which more than one million are impoverished.
The local government of West Bengal and the Central
Government in New Delhi have been struggling to
improve the horrid living conditions in Calcutta's
slums. But, two major hurdles have not been overcome. Firstly, there are more people in Calcutta
than the city could ever absorb within its
boundaries and, secondly, it is impossible to
provide sufficient housing and employment to meet
the overwhelming needs of the slum dwellers.

The only avenue that is open to give the slum
dwellers a chance for a better life for themselves
and their children is to relocate them in less
populated areas of India. Much of India's unused
land in different states could be successfully
irrigated and cultivated. The state government of
West Bengal and the central government can work out

feasible resettlement plans with the other states and offer uncultivated lands and financial incentives to Calcutta's poor to begin new agricultural communities throughout the country. The destitute in Calcutta's slums are both illiterate and unable to move from place to place in search of a job. They will gladly learn new skills and begin a new life elsewhere in India, if they are given proper guidance, financial assistance, and opportunity.

India has been able to absorb an additional 340 million people over the past 35 years. Certainly, the relocation of one million people is not an impossible task. Resettlement programs can be incorporated into India's Five Year Plan. With coordination and planning, the horrible and dehumanizing conditions in which Calcutta's slum dwellers are forced to live can finally be eradicated.

The Indian government initiated family planning in 1952 and was one of the first underdeveloped countries to do so. Because of this, millions of births have been avoided. The following data clearly show that a substantial portion of the federal budget has been allocated to accelerate family planning programs:

First Five Year Plan	–	1,450,000 rupees
Second Five Year Plan	–	21,600,000 rupees
Third Five Year Plan	–	248,600,000 rupees
Fourth Five Year Plan	–	2,844,000,000 rupees
Fifth Five Year Plan	–	4,089,800,000 rupees
Sixth Five Year Plan	–	10,100,000,000 rupees

At present, there is a primary family planning center for every 100,000 people and a subcenter for every 5,000 people. The Sixth Five Year Plan will establish roughly 40,000 additional subcenters during 1980–1985. The World Health Organization, the World Bank, UNICEF, UNFPA, and several other foreign agencies are offering assitance to India in the area of health and family welfare.[17]

The success of family planning in India depends entirely upon the voluntary response of the people. China has succeeded in controlling its population growth by enforcing strict penalties for couples who have more than one child. But such compulsory programs cannot be introduced within the democratic framework. The Indian government has appealed to people to recognize overpopulation as a national problem and to take responsibility for its control by limiting the size of their families.

Family planning has met with some success because Hinduism has no religious doctrines forbidding birth control and each person is free to make a choice on the matter. However, the issue of abortion has definite religious implications for Hindus from the standpoint of the doctrine of karma. Abortion is considered voluntary murder and the law of karma states that individuals are morally accountable for their actions and will suffer for evil deeds in the next reincarnation.

The moral question of abortion can be totally circumvented, however, by the use of reliable contraceptives. Voluntary abstinence from sex cannot be a viable alternative to birth control for India's millions. Along with the practice of spiritual values in marriage and responsible parenthood, one of the foundations of a loving, committed relationship between a man and a woman is the joy of sharing sexual pleasures.

India is primarily a land of villages and the crux of population control revolves around the millions of illiterates and semi-literates living in approximately 576,000 villages. Family planning is popular among educated Indians in urban areas and the movement is very slowly gaining momentum in the villages. Rural Indians do not conceptually understand the dreadful consequences of the population explosion upon India's future generations. Additionally, superstitutions and traditions are deep-rooted among the people. Ironically, the farmers have quickly adapted to new methods of agriculture, such as the use of chemical fertilizers and planting hybrid grains for improved productivity, but birth control has not been received with the same enthusiasm and success. Today, every village family is aware of the fact that family size can be limited and that knowledge is, in itself, a marvelous improvement over the widespread ignorance of family planning methods just 20 years ago.

The Indian government is campaigning very hard to popularize voluntary birth control through radio and television programs, documentaries, newspapers, and billboard advertisements. The study of the population problem has even been introduced in school curriculums. Because food production is increasing faster than the population, India will continue to feed its people in the years to come. But, chronic housing shortages, overcrowded schools and hospitals, inflation, the black market, and high unemployment will continue to escalate and the gap between the rich and the poor will widen even further.

INDIA IN THE YEAR 2000

The topic of what the world situation will be in the year 2000 lends itself to speculative analyses ranging from gloom and doom, with the frightening threat of nuclear annihilation and the destruction of the human race, to optimism that the world will survive unscathed, due to mankind's flexibility in adapting to change and meeting future crises and challenges. Based upon current political, economic and social conditions, the escalating population growth in the underdeveloped nations leaves little room for speculation as to the inevitable disasterous consequences, if the present growth rate continues. Due to increased financial burdens placed upon the underdeveloped nations in Asia, Africa, and Latin America by overpopulation, sustained economic growth cannot be maintained. As a result, many Third World countries will not be able to repay their huge loans to the western financial institutions and the World Bank. Consequently, there is every possibility that the international monetary system will collapse.

As I have already pointed out in the previous chapter, the most crucial and urgent problem which India is facing today is that of overpopulation. It threatens India's social and economic progress and even the democratic foundations of India's political system. Poverty and the need for employment, housing, and health care will continue to escalate in intensity as the years go by and the vide gap between the rich and the poor will further increase. Although India is currently producing sufficient food to feed its growing population, the probability of drought and food shortages in the coming decade cannot be ignored, for Indian agriculture is thoroughly dependent upon the monsoons. Scientists are already predicting uncustomary climatic changes around the world in the next twenty years due to polutants in the atmosphere.

India is endowed with rich natural resources and immense human potential which have not yet been fully utilized. Japan and Germany have achieved tremendous economic success and social prosperity with far less resources and have rebuilt their countries from the rubble of World War II through hard work, self-discipline, determination and ingenuity. India can learn a valuable lesson from the pragmatic approach taken by these two nations.

The future of India can be one of economic prosperity and social progress or economic disaster and social anarchy, depending upon how the government and the people respond to the problems of poverty, unemployment and overpopulation. Through determination, vision and responsible actions carried out by all concerned, India's future can be progressive and prosperous. On the contrary, if callousness, lethargy, corruption, and political infighting predominate, India will definitely face a bleak future. The alternatives are clear-cut and the choice lies with the people.

It is not too late to reshape Indian society by abolishing the evils of casteism and untouchability because spirituality and cultural unity are still alive among the people. The politicians, the educated, businessmen, and religious leaders must all take responsibility in providing strong moral leadership for the good of their communities and the good of the country as a whole. The government alone cannot solve India's multitude of problems. The key to a workable democracy is cooperation through compromise by all segments of the society.

The primary efforts to revitalize the nation should begin with the politicians. Historically, Indian society has functioned well under the guidance of strong administrative leadership, such as that of the Indian monarchs and the colonial rulers. Today, the elected representatives must lead the people with responsibility and commitment.

Unfortunately, politicians in India, for the most part, do not work for the people, rather, they strive toward personal goals and selfish interests. Pre-election slogans are one thing and practical actions after the election are quite a different matter. Corruption and nepotism are spreading like cancer in the society. Innumerable political factions fight among themselves in their struggle for power. Such rivalry has jeopardized major programs which are crucial to the whole country's welfare, such as educating the illiterate masses and controlling the population growth. The main hobby of the Indian politicians seems to be switching political parties at the right time for personal gain and advancement. During the past decade, there has been a mass exodus of politicians from one party to another and then back again to the new party in power. Opposition parties in the parliament literally oppose any new developmental programs which the incumbent party introduces, regardless of the programs' merits. It is no surprise that the people have totally lost trust and confidence in their elected representatives. Unless the politicians reorient their goals and commit themselves to work for their constituencies with integrity and unselfishness, there is little hope that the world's largest democracy will survive. Freedom is a precious heritage and preserving democracy for future generations is the responsibility of all Indians, and, especially, the responsibility of the elected representatives.

The educated people in India can play a vital role in reducing illiteracy in the country through the voluntary organization and support of adult education programs. Whether in cities, towns or villages, the educated can share their reading and writing knowledge with the illiterate by donating a few hours of their time per week to support this endeavor. Additionally, the educated and the businessmen can set up job counseling and placement centers to give creative guidance and encouragement to the unemployed youths.

Indian religious leaders of all denominations are held in great respect and have much influence with their followers because the Indian people still uphold spiritual values as the highest goal in life. Just as Mother Teresa and her Missionaries of Charity are doing marvelous concrete spiritual service in the slums of Calcutta; likewise, Indian religious leaders from all sects can revive spirituality in action by establishing charitable service centers on a non-political, caste-free basis to meet the needs of the poor. Mother Teresa has inspired and touched the hearts of millions of people through her loving service and the religious leaders in India can, through positive action and commitment, revitalize the spirit of moral consciousness, sacrifice and love toward our fellowman. The achievements of the Christian churches in India, both Catholic and Protestant, in serving the people through schools, hospitals, and orphanages, are tremendous. Similarly, the Parsi religious community in Bombay sets a fine example of concrete spiritual service by taking care of the needs of the members of their community. No Parsi beggars can be found in Bombay.

The vast majority of Indians are Hindus but the number of Hindu social service organizations are miniscule when compared to the huge population. Hindu religious leaders can do tremendous spiritual service by establishing centers to help the needy. Likewise, the Hindu religious leaders can exert a powerful influence for positive change in Indian society by reviving the social gospel of dharma and the practice of karma yoga, with emphasis upon brotherhood, morality, and seeking salvation through dedicated, selfless actions.

Unless proper steps are taken now, India will become glutted with people by the year 2000, poverty and hunger will rise to unmanageable proportions, and riots and social anarchy will result. Cities comparable to Calcutta will be found from coast to coast and hundreds of Mother Teresas will be needed to feed the hungry, clothe the naked, and minister to the sick and the dying.

NOTES

Part I: Mother Teresa
1. Calcutta
   1. Mother Teresa's acceptance speech at the presentation of the Pere Marquette Discovery Award, Marquette University, Milwaukee, Wisconsin, June 13, 1981.

2. Mother Teresa
   1. Professor John Sannes' speech at the presentation of the Nobel Peace Prize to Mother Teresa in Oslo, Norway, October 17, 1979.
   2. *Ibid.*
   3. *India-West,* December 14, 1979, p.2.
   4. Nobel Peace Prize acceptance speech by Mother Teresa.
   5. *Ibid.*
   6. Sister Evana is a Yugoslavian missionary who belongs to the Order of the Daughters of the Cross, which has its mother house in Liege, Belgium. She has been serving the poor people in India for the past 50 years and she has been working with the sick and the destitute at Jesu Ashram, Matigara in the Darjeeling District of West Bengal for the past 12 years. A Jesuit brother, Bob Mittelholtz, founded Jesu Ashram to treat the sick, particularly tuberculosis and leprosy patients. The brothers and sisters operate mobile outdoor medical clinics, as well as a free hospital and orphanage, located at Jesu Ashram. Once a week, they join with Mother Teresa's sisters to give medical care to leprosy ptients in the area.

7. "Mother Teresa of Calcutta," *The Monitor*, San Francisco, California, June 10, 1982, p.8.
8. *India-West*, October 19, 1979, p.3.
9. Pere Marquette Discovery Award speech by Mother Teresa.
10. *India: A Reference Annual 1981* (Publication Division, Ministry of Information and Broadcasting, Government of India, December 1981), p.95.
11. "Mother Teresa speaks to City of St. Francis" by Roberta Ward, *The Monitor*, June 10, 1982, p.8.
12. Mother Teresa's speech at St. Mary's Cathedral, San Francisco, California, June 4, 1982.
13. *Ibid.*
14. Pere Marquette Discovery Award speech by Mother Teresa.
15. Mother Teresa's commencement address at Thomas Aquinas College, Santa Paula, California, June 5, 1982.
16. "Mother Teresa speaks to the City of St. Francis" by Roberta Ward, *The Monitor*, June 10, 1982, p.8.
17. Pere Marquette Discovery Award speech by Mother Teresa.
18. Mother Teresa's speech at St. Mary's Cathedral.
19. Pere Marquette Discovery Award speech by Mother Teresa.
20. *Ibid.*
21. "'Be kind, be loving, be thoughtful...know your neighbors'" by Roberta Ward, *The Monitor*, June 10, 1982, p.9.
22. "Reporters question Peace Prize winner," *The Monitor*, June 10, 1982, p.8.
23. Mother Teresa's commencement address at Thomas Aquinas College.

24. "Mother Teresa leaves hope behind for family, city" by Catherine M. Odell, *Our Sunday Visitor*, June 20, 1982, p.3.

25. I*ndia-West*, November 16, 1979, p.3.

26. "Mother Teresa leaves hope behind for family, city" by Catherine M. Odell, *Our Sunday Visitor*, June 20, 1982, p.3.

27. T. S. Eliot, *Selected Essays 1917-1932* (New York: Harcourt Brace, 1932), p.31.

28. Nobel Peace Prize acceptance speech by Mother Teresa.

29. *India-West*, November 16, 1979, p.3.

30. Pere Marquette Discovery Award speech by Mother Teresa.

31. "Mother Teresa in S.F." by Kevin Leary, *San Francisco Chronicle*, June 5, 1982, p.4.

32. "Mother Teresa leaves hope behind for family, city" by Catherine M. Odell, *Our Sunday Visitor*, June 20, 1982, p.3.

33. "Mother Teresa-Can Her Work Survive?" by Marguerite Michaels, *Parade Magazine*, February 21, 1982, p.7.

34. "Mother Teresa speaks to City of St. Francis" by Roberta Ward, *The Monitor*, June 10, 1982, p.8.

35. "Media myth disservice to U.S. nuns" by Dick Ryan, *National Catholic Reporter*, May 28, 1982, p.11.

36. Homily of the Reverend John P. Raynor, S.J., at the presentation of the Pere Marquette Discovery Award to Mother Teresa.

3. Prayer, Poverty and Service
    1. "Reporters question Peace Prize winner," *The Monitor*, June 10, 1982, p.8.
    2. Cf. J.M. Dechenet, *Yoga and God: An Invitation to Christian Yoga* (Abbey Press, St. Meinrad, Indiana, 1975).

3. Nobel Peace Prize acceptance speech by Mother Teresa.

4. "Mother Teresa wins Nobel Prize for Aid to Suffering," *Los Angeles Times*, October 18, 1979, p.6.

5. Nobel Peace Prize acceptance speech by Mother Teresa.

6. "Reporters question Peace Prize winner," *The Monitor*, June 10, 1982, p.8.

7. Mahatma Gandhi, *Harijan*, January 10, 1937, p.5.

4. Shishu Bhavan

   1. "Mother Teresa speaks to City of St. Francis" by Roberta Ward, *The Monitor*, June 10, 1982, p.8.

   2. *Ibid.*

   3. I*bid.*

   4. Elizabeth Browning, "The Cry of the Children," *The Complete Poetical Works of Elizabeth Barrett Browning*, Cambridge Edition (New York: Houghton Mifflin Co., 1900), pp.156-158.

   5. "Female Fetus Abortions Big Business, Threatens India's Population Ratio" by Najmul Hasan, *India-West*, July 30, 1982, p.16.

5. Nirmal Hriday

   1. "Poverty, chastity, obedience extolled," *The Monitor*, June 10, 1982, p.9.

   2. "'Be kind, be loving, be thoughtful...know your neighbors'" by Roberta Ward, *The Monitor*, June 10, 1982, p.9.

   3. Asato Ma Sadgamaya
      Tamaso Ma Jyotirgamaya
      Mrtyo Ma Amrtamgamaya.
      Brihadaranyaka Upanishad, 1.3.28

   4. Abinash Chandra Bose, *Hymns from the Vedas* (Asia Publishing House, Bombay, 1966), p.357.

Part II: India

7. A Glimpse of Hinduism

1. *Chandogya Upanishad*, 6.1.1-3. Translated by Robert Ernest Hume, *The Thirteen Principal Upanishads*, Second Edition, Revised (Oxford University Press, 1949).

2. *Katha Upanishad*, 3.3.6. Quoted in C. Rajagopalachari, *Hinduism* (Bharatiya Vidya Bhavan, Bombay, 1964), p.53.

3. *Katha Upanishad*, 3.10, Hume translation.

4. *Katha Upanishad*, 1.3.12. Quoted in C. Rajagopalachari, *Hinduism* (Bharatiya Vidya Bhavan, Bombay, 1964), p.113.

5. *Brihadaranyaka Upanishad*, III.VII.23. Translated by Swami Madhavananda, *The Brihadaranyaka Upanishad* (Advaita Ashram, Calcutta, 1969).

6. Song of Tukaram. Translated by John S. Hoyland, *An Indian Peasant Mystic* (Allenson and Co., London, 1932).

7. *The Bhagavad Gita*, 4.11.

8. *Ibid.*, 9.30.

9. *Ibid.*, 12.8.

10. *Ibid.*, 4.7-8.

11. *Ibid.*, 2.47.

12. *Ibid.*, 3.19.

13. *Ibid.*, 9.27-28.

14. "Reporters question Peace Prize winner," *The Monitor*, June 10, 1982, p.8.

15. Heinrich Zimmer, *The Philosophies of India* (Princeton University Press, Princeton, New Jersey, 1969), p.163.

16. *The Mahabharata*, 109.11-12.

17. *Ibid.*, 109.10.

18. *The Mahabharata*, 3.31. Edited by Pratapchandra Roy (Oriental Publishing Company, Calcutta).

19. *Brihadaranyaka Upanishad*, 4.4.5.

20. *Shankara's Commentary on Brihadaranyaka Upanishad*, IV.4.22.
21. K.V. Rangaswami Aiyangar, *Aspects of Ancient Indian Economic Thought*, Benares, p.31.
22. *Purusharthasudhanidhi of Shankaracharya*, 1.1.1.
23. *Anguttara-Nikaya II. Pattakammavagga*, 6.2.3.
24. *Panchatantra.* Translated by Arthur M. Ryder (Jaico Publishing House, Bombay, 1949), pp.207-208.
25. *Ibid.*, p.219.
26. *Kama Sutra*, 1.2.11.
27. *The Mahabharata*, 75.49.
28. Kautilya, *Artha Shastra*, 1.7.
29. *The Collected Works of Mahatma Gandhi* (Publications Division, Ministry of Information and Broadcasting, Government of India), Vol. 10, p.58.
30. *Manusmriti*, IV.12.
31. *Brihadaranyaka Upanishad*, 4.4.7.

8. Social Problems of India

1. *Rig Veda*, 10.10.12.
2. *Satapata Brahmana*, II.2.2.6.
3. *Vishnu Dharma Sutra*, 19.20
4. *The Collected Works of Mahatma Gandhi*, Vol. 21, p.197.
5. *Ibid.*, Vol. 17, p.534.
6. *Ibid.*, Vol. 19, p.513.
7. *Ibid.*, Vol. 56, p.47.
8. *Harijan*, March 6, 1939.
9. Dhananjay Keer, *Dr. Ambedkar, Life and Mission* (A.V. Keer, Bombay, 1953), p.162.
10. Cf. *India: A Reference Annual 1981*, p.118.
11. Cf. *Caste and Social Stratification Among Muslims in India.* Edited by Imtiaz Ahmad (South Asia Books, Columbia, Missouri, 1978).

12. *Cf. India: A Reference Annual 1981*,
    pp.117-128.
13. *The Hindu*, Madras, May 22, 1971.
14. *Bhavan's Journal*, Bombay, May 13, 1962.
15. S. Chandrashekar, *The Untouchables in
    Contemporary India*.   Edited by Michael
    Mahar (The University of Arizona Press,
    Tucson, Arizona, 1972), p. xxvii.
16. *Cf. India: A Reference Annual 1981*, pp.
    193-196.
17. *Ibid.*, pp.104-107.